Reward Systems:
Does Yours Measure Up?

Manage the Media
(Don't Let the Media Manage You)
by William J. Holstein, award-winning writer for the
New York Times, Fortune, and *Barron's*

Strategic Alliances: Three Ways to Make Them Work
by Steve Steinhilber, Vice President of Strategic Alliances
at Cisco Systems

Succession: Are You Ready?
by Marshall Goldsmith, bestselling author of
What Got You Here Won't Get You There

Reward Systems: Does Yours Measure Up?

Steve Kerr
with Glenn Rifkin

Harvard Business Press

Boston, Massachusetts

ISBN 978-1-4221-1911-2

Library-of-Congress cataloging information forthcoming

The paper used in this publication meets the requirements of the American
National Standard for Permanence of Paper for Publications and Documents
in Libraries and Archives Z39.48-1992.

Contents

The Power of Reward Systems

There are problems in the business world—for example, computer viruses—that people would pay a great deal to solve but for which no one has a solution. There are other problems—like providing top-quality health care to all employees—whose solutions are well known but so expensive that most organizations can't afford to solve them. There are also problems—like putting out the monthly payroll—whose solutions are well known and affordable; but because they're well known and affordable, everyone is doing them well, so there's no competitive advantage in doing them well. And then there are reward systems. The basic principles behind a successful reward system are as well known as putting out the monthly payroll, and doing it well is actually less expensive than doing it poorly. Yet these principles are usually violated, even by managers who perform their other duties competently. Therefore, there's a huge competitive advantage to be had by doing it well.

When Reward Systems Go Wrong

On the other hand, getting reward systems wrong almost always produces expensive, and unwanted, results. For instance, although the U.S. health care system is the most expensive in the world, Americans are far from the world's healthiest people. In part, this is due to flawed incentives. Consider this: physicians can err in either of two ways. They can diagnose a well patient as sick, thus causing needless anxiety and expense, curtailment of favorite foods and activities, and even physical danger by subjecting him to unnecessary medications or surgery. Conversely, they can pronounce a sick person well, preventing him from seeking medical attention that might cure him.

We want physicians to minimize both types of errors, but studies show that healthy patients are far more likely to be told they are ill than sick patients are to be diagnosed as healthy. One important reason is that labeling someone healthy who turns out to be sick can be embarrassing and legally risky, whereas calling a healthy person sick is often dismissed as good conservative medicine. Doctors also know they will never be sued for the useless tests they do perform but may well be sued for the useless tests they don't perform. Healthy patients are also a good source of continuing business, who will not embarrass the doctor by dying abruptly.

Hospitals are also encouraged to engage in undesirable behaviors. For example, because they are rewarded in a variety of ways for having high patient recovery rates, many hospitals prefer to admit relatively healthy patients, and some hospitals have achieved notoriety by turning away people who were desperately in need of care. Hospitals are also rewarded for admitting people who could be treated more efficiently as outpatients, running up the bills during their stay and delaying (or expediting) their discharge for economic rather than medical reasons. Another problem is that hospitals either aren't reimbursed at all for preventive care or get much less than they receive for treating existing symptoms. Insurance companies inadequately reimburse preventive medicine not because they fail to understand its importance but because the reward systems they are subjected to make it unprofitable for them to do so. As a result of these and other anomalies, only 7 percent of the money expended on U.S. health care in 2007 went for prevention. If an ounce of prevention is worth a pound of cure—well, you do the math.

Flawed reward systems have also worked against national interests in times of war. At the risk of oversimplifying, let's assume that the primary wartime goal of most military organizations is to win the war. Let's further assume that the primary goal of most combatants is to get home, alive and in one piece. These circumstances have the potential to create an acute misalignment of goals, in that rational behavior by members of the military will prevent that military organization from accomplishing its primary objective.

But not necessarily! It depends on the reward system. For example, the Vietnam War featured numerous reported incidents of American soldiers "fragging" (i.e., killing their own commanding officer because he had volunteered his unit for dangerous missions), "search and evade," mutiny, desertion, and other acts of disobedience. World War II, on the other hand, generated far fewer reported incidents of this kind. Many factors contributed to these differences, but it's instructive to examine a key difference in the reward systems. What did the American soldier in World War II want? To go home. When did he get to go home? When the war was won. While he waited to go home he was subjected to severe penalties for refusing to obey orders. As a result of the reward system, most American participants in World War II, whether patriotic or not, considered it to be in their own best interest to do their part to win the war.

Now, what did the American soldier in Vietnam want? To go home. When did he go home? When his rotational tour of duty was over, whether or not the war was won. Because it was politically necessary to distribute the risks of combat, the reward system in Vietnam emphasized equity at the expense of efficiency. It also became evident that deserters and mutineers were more likely to be granted rest and rehabilitation (on the assumption that fatigue drove them to these measures) than to suffer major negative consequences. As a result, many American combatants concluded that working to help win the war was not to their personal advantage.

More recently, in Iraq, the U.S. Army again installed a rotational system. But in the absence of a draft, manpower was limited, so some units were sent back to Iraq after their tours of duty were over and others were told just before heading home that their tours had been extended. Ironically, for many Americans, a system that had been devised to sacrifice efficiency for equity ended up providing neither.

In these two examples—health care and military operations—people's lives literally depend on the effectiveness of the organization's reward systems. Even if the stakes at your organization aren't quite so high, poor incentive structures can still cost you dearly.

Using the Reward System to Get What You Want

Most businesses are replete with undesirable behaviors that stem from disregarding the fundamental principles of organizational reward systems. Table 1 introduces some common dysfunctions, along with their predictable consequences. (All these dysfunctions will be discussed in greater detail later, along with suggestions about how they can be prevented.)

A defining characteristic of any good reward system is that it gets you what you want. Maybe you're a big fan of the behaviors described in table 1. My guess, however, is that those are the kinds of behaviors that drive you crazy, and you'd put a stop to them if you could. Actually, there's an excellent chance you can, but the first step in solving any problem is to define it correctly. To most managers it seems obvious that the fault lies with those employees who are deceiving their boss, manipulating their numbers, and competing with their colleagues. I will argue in this book that that perspective oversimplifies the problem, tantamount to what B. F. Skinner has labeled "blaming the rat."

Skinner coined the term to describe the frustration he felt in the early days of his career when he

6

TABLE 1

Dysfunctional behaviors resulting from faulty reward systems

Organizations want	But tend to reward	So often get
Long-term growth	Employees who achieve quarterly targets	Overemphasis on short-term performance, employees who game the numbers
Innovative products, new ideas	Employees who don't make mistakes	Risk-averse behavior
Interunit cooperation, teamwork	Individual goal attainment	Self-serving activities, unproductive competition
Candor, bad news to surface, people to provide honest feedback	Employees who avoid delivering the tough messages	People who shoot the messenger, employees who agree with their boss, performance appraisals that rate everyone above average
Performance	Attendance	Employees who come in on time and look busy
World-class client service	Operating and cost efficiencies	"Your call is very important to us, so please stay on the line . . ."

would run experiment after experiment and his rats wouldn't do what he wanted. He recalled screaming at them, "Why don't you behave? Behave as you ought!" Later on, he reports, he had a painful insight: his rats were behaving! He had been designing his experiments poorly, and his rats were responding rationally to a flawed reward system. Once he got his reinforcement contingencies to function properly, his rats became predictable and controllable. It seems bizarre to imagine a distinguished scientist screaming at his laboratory animals, but that's not very different from what many senior executives do. They (inadvertently and often unknowingly) devise reward systems that discourage the behaviors they want and reward the very actions that drive them crazy.

"Blaming the rat" underlies this book's most important purpose, which is change your definition of the problem. Instead of saying, "My people aren't motivated and it's not my fault," you'll say, "My people—at least, the great majority of them—aren't to blame for the things they do that I don't like; it's my reward (and measurement) systems that are at fault." Viewed through this lens, the bad news is that *you* are responsible for the dysfunctional behaviors that so bother you. Like Skinner's insight, this is painful. But the good news is that if you're causing it, you can fix it—and without adding head count, upgrading IT capabilities, engaging consultants, or altering the personalities of your people.

This book tells you how.

The Three Steps to Getting Reward Systems Right

Since 1970 I have spent thirteen years as chief learning officer (CLO) for GE and Goldman Sachs; twenty-three years on the faculties of Ohio State, the University of Southern California, and the University of Michigan; and three years as a business consultant. (So it is not surprising that most of the examples in this book come from business and academic institutions. However, to demonstrate the universality of the principles of reward and measurement and the consequences of violating them, I have included a number of examples from sports, health care, politics, and other venues.)

In addition to being CLO, I was General Electric's head of leadership development for seven years during Jack Welch's tenure as CEO, including responsibility for GE's leadership development center at Crotonville. During my time with GE, I hosted senior leaders from hundreds of companies and spoke to numerous executive teams about the systems, processes, and values of the company. Many of my guests were particularly interested in GE's approach to setting goals, monitoring progress, and motivating and rewarding its employees. To get my guests thinking, I would often begin by saying, "My job this morning is to unimpress you. You're not going to hear me brag about our superior IT systems, our army of consultants, or our secret theories of motivation, because we don't have any of those things. I'm also not going to tell you how to spend large sums of money you probably don't have. What we do well at GE are the basics." The basics were three things:

1. Operationally defining what we meant by performance—converting our values, mission statements, and strategies into tangible goals (including stretch goals) and then converting those goals into actions

2. Devising comprehensive metrics that tracked our actions and assessed progress toward our goals

3. Creating financial and nonfinancial reward systems that met employees' needs, reinforced our metrics, and aligned the company's goals with the work our people were doing

Although only one of those points explicitly refers to rewards, together they constitute the three key components of an effective reward system. Each is essential in its own right, but it's equally important that they be addressed in that particular sequence. This means that rewards must be the third thing you work on. Metrics come second. Defining performance, and making your definition operational, must come first. If there are things you'd like your people to do that you think can't be rewarded, you're wrong, because anything that can be measured can be rewarded. If you'd like some things done that you think are impossible to measure, you're wrong again. You've probably neglected to operationally define what you want, because anything that can be described in actionable terms can be measured.

The purpose of this book is to enable you to excel in these three vitally important areas.

Step 1: Define Performance in Actionable Terms

Some mission statements are deliberately designed to be so broad, vague, and socially desirable that it is impossible to be against them. Their purpose is not to drive action, and in fact, one of their principal virtues is that no one can figure out what actions are being planned, what alternative goals will be ignored, or where the money will come from. Their aim is to elicit warm, unfocused feelings of goodwill toward the statement or its author. These statements are the typical stock-in-trade for the politician who hopes to gain your support while committing himself to nothing that restricts his future flexibility. This book is intended not for those politicians but for you—whose vision, mission, and goals strive to define purpose and catalyze behavior. For these mission statements to do their job, however, they must be actionable.

Consider the following two statements: "We intend to triple our revenue by the year 2012" and

"We want to be the best business in the whole wide world." Although these two statements may seem to exemplify very different approaches to articulating a mission, they suffer from the same defects. First, since there is no way to be opposed to statements of this kind, no one will oppose them, making it impossible to know whether your people really embrace what you are trying to accomplish. Second, it's impossible to determine from these statements what anyone is supposed to do to support the objective. Third, the vagueness of both statements makes it hard to measure the organization's progress toward the objective and to assess the performance of individual employees. Finally, setting forth visions and mission statements in such a manner affords you no competitive advantage, because nobody can distinguish your vacuous statements from everyone else's.

To illustrate this last point, when I taught in the University of Michigan's executive programs, I would ask participants to place their value and mission statements in a shoe box at the front of the room. I would then say, "I'm going to randomly select a statement and read a few sentences from the middle of the page. If it's yours, raise your hand." In a typical session, when I started reading three hands would go up—belonging to an exporter, someone from the U.S. Coast Guard, and a urinal manufacturer. All three thought I was reading their mission statement! Sometimes I would ask each participant to write on her statement the approximate number of hours that had gone into its preparation. The numbers were often depressingly large—175 hours, 220 hours, 400 hours— yet these executives couldn't tell their own mission statements from the urinal manufacturer's.

To make this point when I speak to executives who all work for the same firm, I sometimes show them this code of ethics statement and ask them whose it is:

We are responsible for conducting [our] business affairs in accordance with all applicable
laws and in a moral and honest manner . . .
We want to be proud of [our company] and
to know that it enjoys a reputation for fairness
and honesty and that it is respected.

Some people invariably think it's their own. Others imagine it to be from Johnson & Johnson, GE, or one of the other organizations known to take such things seriously—but it's actually from Enron. Enron's motto, by the way, was "respect, integrity, communication, and excellence." Enron's words were as inspirational as everyone else's; its actions, however, were not.

Such exercises show how hard it is to differentiate your own organization by virtue of your description of it. All the good words have already been taken; the key to distinctiveness lies in how people in your organization behave. Nordstrom built its reputation for customer service, for example, not via mission statements and slogans but through its hassle-free response to customer returns and *non*customer returns; by being willing to take back merchandise that didn't come from one of its stores. Similarly, there is nothing original about the lofty promises of the U.S. Army to transform enlistees into leaders; however, the organization's behavior in this area, notably its mentoring practices and after-action reviews, have earned it a great reputation for leadership development.

The Bull's-Eye Exercise

One very effective tool to make visions, missions, goals, and priorities actionable is the bull's-eye exercise, so named because it is depicted as a three-ringed target. (See figure 1.) In the outer ring go the goals and initiatives you are trying to make actionable— for example, diversity, empowerment, teamwork, globalization, or customer satisfaction. In the inner-most ring goes the output of the exercise—that is, descriptions of specific employee behaviors that are deemed necessary to achieve the desired outcomes. Participants in the exercise (who can be anyone from

FIGURE 1

The bull's-eye exercise: Making mission, vision, and principles actionable

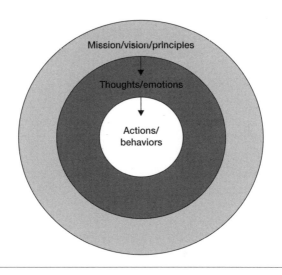

Mission/vision/principles

Thoughts/emotions

Actions/behaviors

your management committee to middle- and low-level employees) are asked to imagine themselves at a party a year from now, held to celebrate the remarkable progress your organization has made toward the stated goal. At this imaginary party, your people are asked to identify the behavior changes—in themselves and other employees—that have made your organization so much more global, team oriented, client centered, or whatever, than it was a year ago.

Specifically, you ask, "What are people doing more of than they were a year ago, and what are they doing less of?"

The middle ring between the outer circle and the bull's-eye itself reflects the fact that as people begin to identify behaviors, they usually go through an intermediate stage in which they find themselves describing thoughts and emotions instead of actual behaviors. For example, when asked what would change to improve a firm's branding initiative, one team replied, "More respect for our products and services." This is probably accurate, but respect is a "thought" word, not a behavior. Another team, asked what would have to change to better its empowerment program, said that there would be "less employee fear." This is also accurate, but fear is an emotion, not a behavior. When responses describe thoughts or emotions, ask this follow-up question: "If the workforce had more respect (or less fear), what would people *do* that they're not doing now?" Primed in this manner, most people have no trouble hitting the bull's-eye, and after a few experiences with the technique, most groups find it to be an easy and enjoyable exercise.

One interesting pattern I've observed as a result of putting numerous teams through the bull's-eye exercise is that employees almost always identify a greater number of "more of" than "less of" items.

Usually, however, the "less of" entries generate the most emotion. Sometimes your employees can't fully articulate what new behaviors are required for your change effort to be successful, but they can sure tell you what behaviors have to stop!

In addition to making your goals, missions, and values actionable, the bull's-eye exercise provides these additional advantages.

Testing employee buy-in. I noted earlier that vision and mission statements tend to be cast in such syrupy terms that no one can be against them. Slogans such as "strive to be the best," "make growth happen," and "delight your customers" invariably receive 100 percent buy-in, perhaps because your employees are beguiled by the words without a clear sense of what you mean. By converting your words into desired actions, you'll get a true test of whether your people really support the initiatives.

Creating more effective delegation. This exercise lays a firm groundwork for delegation by making the bull's-eye at each organizational level the top ring of the bull's-eye at the level directly beneath it. This process is sometimes referred to as "cascading." You and your management committee, for example, may set a 12 percent improvement goal for top-line growth next year. Committee members may believe, and so would enter in their bulls-eye, that three things must be done to achieve this goal: develop fresh new products, improve market research, and put better-trained salespeople in the field. If I'm your head of leadership development, you probably won't mention new products and better marketing to me, but I'll put your statement about better-trained salespeople into the outer ring of my bull's-eye exercise. When I meet with my team, we may conclude that to have better-trained salespeople in the field, we need to update the firm's sales training curriculum. That idea, entered in my bull's-eye, will then go into my training manager's top ring, and so on down the line.

My experience has been that in organizations where decisions tend to be imposed from the top, the bull's-eye exercise forces a certain degree of empowerment, by allowing employees to identify activities and set targets in their areas of specialty—provided, of course, that their efforts align with the goals and priorities established higher up. Conversely, in organizations that tend to pursue consensus to a fault, continually revisiting decisions already made, the exercise provides discipline by ensuring that the outer rings established at higher levels will be honored. (In my example, although I would be encouraged to make full use of my judgment and expertise, I would not be expected to challenge the management committee's conclusion that the firm needs better-trained salespeople in the field.)

Laying the groundwork for other organizational processes. A central premise of this book is that the quality of your rewards and metrics depends greatly on how well performance is defined and made operational. Let me note here that selection, training, and most of your other organizational processes are also strongly dependent on your definition of performance.

Having spoken about the bulls-eye technique in general terms, let's now take a look at three real-world examples of the exercise in action.

Example 1: "Empowerment"

In the early days of GE's Work-Out program, some business unit managers were so eager to support the program that they pushed the concept of empowerment to dysfunctional extremes—pandering to their subordinates, approving bad ideas, and so on. It got to the point where GE's CEO, Jack Welch, told the Work-Out consultants that we might have to stop using the term *empowerment* altogether. We suggested instead that we make the concept actionable,

using the bull's-eye exercise to create a shared under-
standing of what it means, behaviorally, to be an
empowering leader. Here are a few of the behaviors
we came up with that were subsequently incorporated into Crotonville's leadership curriculum:

- When someone comes to you for a signature
  or an approval, you should count the number
  of people who have already signed off. If
  the number is two or more, you should ask
  yourself, "Why am I signing this? What value
  am I adding?" We took the view that once
  three people have thought about something,
  additional layers of approval were not adding
  control and accountability but diluting it.
  We made some bad decisions and had a
  scandal or two during my years with GE,
  and in no case did the problem turn out
  to be too few signatures on some piece of
  paper.

- When someone comes to you for a decision,
  you should ask yourself, "What keeps him
  from making that decision without my help?"
  If the answer is that you have information he
  doesn't have, you should explore the possibility
  that he can get the information directly and
  make the decision.

- When someone comes to you for a signature or an approval, you should ask yourself, "When's the last time I reversed one of these?" If the answer is seldom or never, you should again ask, "Why am I signing this? What value am I adding?" We had well-paid, competent heads of HR, for example, signing off on employees' tuition remissions. We asked, "When's the last time you reversed one?" And they said, "Never. It would be illegal to reverse one. The employment contract says that if an employee pursues a degree from an approved college and maintains at least a B average, the company will pay a specified portion of the tuition."

Do you see the difference the bull's-eye exercise can make? If I asked whether your organization would benefit from greater empowerment, you'd find it difficult to respond, and if you were to set an objective to get greater empowerment, it would be hard to determine whether progress was being made. However, if I asked whether the empowerment behaviors described in Crotonville's leadership curriculum would benefit your firm, you could make a much more informed response, and if you did implement them, it would be relatively easy to assess whether your people were delegating more decisions, requiring fewer signatures, and so forth.

Example 2: "Teamwork"

Teamwork is at the heart of GE's culture, and on the employee self-evaluations, nearly everyone described themselves as being good team players. Viewed from the corporate center, however, many people were overly focused on making their own numbers rather than the company's and were competing with employees who worked in other departments. To address this problem, we decided to define teamwork so radically that no one could claim to be behaving that way. Here's what we came up with:

teamwork = not permitting others to fail.

Then, using the bull's-eye exercise (with "not permitting others to fail" in the top circle), we asked employees to imagine themselves at a party a year later, held to celebrate the fact that people were now behaving in accordance with the definition.

Here are a few of the many behaviors that were identified as a result of the exercise:

- "Enable the other GE businesses to extend credit to their best customers at lower-than-market rates, through financing provided by GE Capital" (proposed by GE Capital)

- "Permit the other GE businesses to invite their best customers to commute between events on the NBC yacht during the Sydney Olympics" (suggested by NBC)

- "Share best practices with the other GE businesses with respect to how we organized and manage our best-in-class accounts receivable process (and our mentoring program and our technical library)"

Example 3: "Common Coffeepot"

When I took over as head of leadership development for GE, Welch met with me to discuss my new job and then ended our meeting by saying, "Here's what I want from you. I want Crotonville to be the common coffeepot of this company." He said this as though I was supposed to know what it meant. (I didn't.) This kind of directive—reminiscent of a mission statement that has not been made operational—is sometimes referred to as "glop from the top." I don't mean this as a criticism. I was an officer of the company, and the CEO had every right to expect me to figure out how to make his directive actionable. My response was to call my new staff together and take them through the bull's-eye exercise, with the words *common coffeepot* in the outer ring.

As an example of how the process worked, one behavior we identified was that Crotonville's courses should not be offered to individual GE businesses but only to multiple businesses attending at the same time. However, one of the GE businesses in Thailand asked us to reconsider, because management there couldn't find local vendors to deliver the desired content. We resolved the problem by agreeing to develop a course for that business, and its leaders agreed to make half the seats in the organization's classroom available to the other GE businesses in Thailand and to help market the course to these other businesses.

In addition to the advantages of the bull's-eye technique already mentioned, it's a wonderful "glop deflector," permitting you to convert even the most Zen-like directives into actions. The exercise doesn't ensure that the behaviors you come up with will be the right ones, but at least it gives you something to take to your boss or to the board. In this example, I was able to go back to Welch and say, "Before I implement my plan to make Crotonville the common coffeepot of the company, I thought you might like to see what my team and I intend to do"—a more elegant conversation starter, you will agree, than "Sir, I have no idea what you're talking about."

How Many Goals Should You Set?

Most management texts and consultants caution that it's important not to set too many goals—that doing so will cause you to lose focus, spend all your time fussing with your metrics, and indicate to your people that no goal is really important.

This is bad advice, and you shouldn't take it. The truth is that it isn't up to you. You must discover how many goals to set. Every organization has stakeholders whose support you need to survive and prosper. Particulars vary, but in general, investors and creditors give you initial capital, customers give you replacement capital, employees contribute labor, suppliers furnish materials, and the government grants you permission to be in business. These folks are not particularly altruistic; they want things from you and get cranky if they don't get them. What's more, no virtuous circle exists to cause the things they want to be compatible with each other and synergistic with your company's priorities. If you have marginal dollars left over, your employees would enjoy a holiday bonus, shareholders would welcome a dividend increase, customers would appreciate a price break, and the EPA would really like you to do something about the gray stuff behind your plant that appears to be glowing. You can't fully please all these folks (or any of them, for that matter), but you'd better find the wherewithal to give each of them at least the minimum necessary to keep them in the game. If you don't, your best employees will quit, your customers will buy from someone else, your shareholders will sell and drive your share price down, and the government will come up with things that are even more unpleasant.

Even if each stakeholder wants only three things from you—and typically they want a lot more than that—you will need to set fifteen, eighteen, twenty-one goals or more, depending on how many stakeholders you have. Do I wish the number was less than that—maybe three to five, as many consultants recommend? I do. I'm convinced that if my boss asked me to do only a few things, I would do them really well. And do I wish stakeholders were more reasonable? I do. I wish I could say to the nice people at the EPA, "We don't like that gray stuff any more than you do, but we're launching some exciting customer initiatives this quarter. Come September, we're on it!"

Of course, it's true that goals (and metrics) can be stacked, chunked, and aggregated to reduce their overall number. It's also true that not all goals need to constitute aggressive improvements above present levels. If your stakeholders are content with your current level of performance and you are, too, you can set maintenance objectives for those areas and focus your attention elsewhere. And of course, no single individual or department needs to be tasked with all your goals. The CEO may worry about all eighteen, for example; the CFO, fifteen; the head of HR, nine; and the clerk in the mail room, only two. Collectively, however, if your stakeholders require you to do eighteen things well, the number of goals you set had better be at least eighteen.

The Use of Stretch Goals

Someone once noted that most people don't aim too high and miss; they aim too low and hit. Easy goals tend to demotivate people, as evidenced by research that shows that most people attain easy goals but don't greatly exceed them. When goals are set to mildly upgrade existing performance, people unconsciously restrict their thinking to solutions that are not very different from prevailing practices. Stretch goals, on the other hand, are so far beyond current levels that they force people to seek radically new solutions. Since stretch goals are so aggressive, they are often skeptically received—as they should be, since most of them won't be met. This was deeply troubling to GE, because its culture is built around strong expectations of success. The company prides itself on being a strict meritocracy, with attractive rewards going to employees who succeed and little forgiveness for those who fail. Yet GE knew that taking a hard line toward people who miss their stretch goals would be unfair and demotivating. To guard against overreacting to failure, we began to teach in Crotonville that to assess performance on stretch goals, managers should take three things into account:

- What impact has the stretch goal had on performance?

- How does our performance in the area of the stretch goal compare to our competitors' performance?

- If the stretch target has not actually been met, has meaningful progress toward it been made?

Through these questions, GE was able to maintain its meritocratic culture without creating performance tests that most people were bound to fail.

When setting stretch goals, particular attention must focus on the extent to which organizational units are interdependent. For example, if sales sets a stretch goal concerning the number of units to be sold, manufacturing must make a decision about how many units to produce. Normally, production levels are driven by the sales projections, but manufacturing knows that sales's stretch goal is unlikely to be achieved and doesn't want to get stuck with additional inventory. On the other hand, by setting production levels too low, manufacturing may ruin whatever chance sales does have to succeed.

One final point is worth making. Of course, it's important to do one's best to resolve these issues. Remember, though, that the specific targets the stretch goals articulate are ultimately much less important than the energy and activity they stimulate and their effectiveness in getting people to conceive of their jobs in new, innovative ways. We knew that most of the stretch goals would not be achieved, and indeed, if any business unit had achieved most of them, we would have become suspicious about the quality of the goals they were setting. However, although the majority of stretch goals were not attained, it soon became clear to us that stretch goals usually triggered performance levels well above what we would have received without them—and that was the metric we cared most about.

Step 2: Devise Comprehensive Metrics

Rewards are easy to get excited about. Most people hear far too much about the goodies everybody else seems to be getting—bonuses, stock options, runaway CEO compensation, and the like—so when a consultant offers to bring your reward system into the twenty-first century, he usually gets a friendly reception. Measurement is a different story. Chances are, your organization has revamped its performance appraisal and review systems more than once in recent years with no discernible gain in employee satisfaction, and most people have little interest in going another round. That's too bad, because starting at the wrong end—adding to the power of your reward system before upgrading your metrics—is a big mistake.

Measuring Things Right

I previously underscored the point that the quality of your metrics rests heavily on how well you have defined performance. In the same way, the strength of your reward system depends greatly on the competence of your metrics. You should think of your metrics as a table that supports the weight of your reward system. Some organizations have rewards that are so light (i.e., so meager, so unattractive, or so unrelated to performance) that employees don't much worry about how favorably they're evaluated. As you make your rewards more attractive, you put more strain on your metrics. To demonstrate this point, I would tell my class near semester's end, "While you've been studying me, I've been studying you, and I'm now prepared to name this year's outstanding student. It's—Lois! And what Lois wins is a volume of the collected speeches of Steve Kerr. What's your reaction?" And they would say, "Congratulations, Lois"; "Way to go, Lois"; "You deserve it!" However, if I changed the prize to something worthwhile, their response invariably was, "Why Lois? What did she do that I didn't do? It should have been me."

Here's an illustration of what can happen when you seek to enhance your reward system before your metrics are in order. When Jimmy Carter was president of the United States, he sought to install a merit pay system for civil service employees. The plan was soon abandoned, because it quickly became evident that no reliable metrics existed to determine which civil servants were meritorious. Carter didn't ruin the measurement system. It was never any good, and so long as raises and promotions were based on seniority and examinations, the question of competence never arose. By seeking to make rewards contingent on performance, Carter put more weight on the measurement system than it could bear.

As these illustrations show, flaws in your measurement system often don't show up until you upgrade your rewards. This causes many managers to falsely conclude that the problem rests with the rewards themselves. For example, a Goldman Sachs client recently lamented that his firm, built on a foundation of humility, seemed to have strayed from its roots. "And of course," he concluded, "you can't reward people for being humble." "Sure you can," I replied, unhelpfully. "Here's what you do: treat your humble people to a paid vacation in Hawaii. Humble people like to go to Hawaii." I was trying to make the point that, although he thought of it as a reward problem, the real issue was that the firm had not developed a metric for humility.

The importance of measurement is nicely captured in the adage "Management gets what it inspects, not what it expects." If something isn't measured, you can't give people feedback about it, so they can't improve. You can't reward the people who are doing it well, and you can't improve or admonish people who do it poorly. Measurement also signals that something is important; if no one is tracking it, it will take a backseat to things that are being scrutinized.

When designing a competent measurement system, one must often choose between attributes that are desirable but inherently contradictory. Three of the most important trade-offs are discussed next.

Trade-off 1: Control Versus Development

Among the most important purposes of measurement is improving future performance. I've noted that if performance data are lacking, good feedback is impossible, and lacking feedback, future performance cannot improve. However, accurate information about prior performance doesn't necessarily lead to improved performance. In some cases requisite skills are lacking. Another key factor concerns how open the recipient is to the data, particularly negative data, he receives. Openness, in turn, is influenced by how the information is presented, the ground rules concerning its use, and who else will see it.

One way to dramatically increase an employee's receptivity to negative information is to use the information for developmental purposes only, by establishing a procedure whereby each employee receives information about his own performance but the employee's manager only gets aggregate data about all the employees in her unit. Under these conditions, employees are more likely to select appropriate people to conduct their 360-degree appraisals, instead of omitting the toughest critics. Reviewers are more likely to be candid, knowing their comments will not get anyone in trouble. Most important, recipients of negative feedback are far more likely to accept and act on it when they know that it is intended for their benefit, rather than to justify failing to promote them or giving them smaller raises.

Unfortunately, under these ground rules, the data cannot be used to inform decisions about promotions, terminations, salary increases, and job assignments, thus greatly impairing the quality of these decisions. Furthermore, without information from peers and subordinates, such important aspects of performance as teamwork, mentoring, and humane treatment of subordinates cannot be measured and so will not be rewarded.

Fortunately, your performance data *can* be used for both control and development—just not at the same time. The right answer is to use the data solely for developmental purposes at first but, after some specified period, to begin to collect information that will be used for evaluation and control. Here's an example: during my tenure as dean of the faculty at the University of Southern California (USC) business school, we were required to be reviewed every fifth year by our accrediting organization, the Association to Advance Collegiate Schools of Business (AACSB). We knew that the information the AACSB garnered in year five would be used for formal evaluation purposes, with high costs to us if it didn't like what it saw. But in year five, with so much at stake, we made every effort to present ourselves in a good light by defending and minimizing our weaknesses. In year four the AACSB would brief us on each of the metrics we would be evaluated against during the following year. The information we obtained that year through self-study did not have to be shared with anyone outside our school. Needless to say, the greatest improvement our school made was in year four. However, had a formal review not been scheduled for the following year, we might never have got around to acting on the self-study information.

Some departments in Goldman Sachs use a similar approach to resolving the control versus development dilemma, through a developmental review in midyear and then a formal review, with fewer restrictions on how the information is used, at year's end. Akin to the published experiences of other firms, Goldman has found that peers and subordinates are more candid, and the subject of the feedback more receptive to criticism, when they know that the data will not factor into discussions on pay and promotions. Goldman has found that bosses, too, are more candid. Furthermore, Goldman discovered that bosses are also more honest in the year-end reviews, perhaps feeling that, since prior friendly warnings had been ineffective, it was time to attach some consequences to their dissatisfaction.

Trade-off 2: Rating Versus Ranking

Though they are described in numerous ways, there are only two types of measurement systems—rating and ranking. Rating systems compare people (or organizations) to articulated standards. In kindergarten, if you worked and played well with others, you received high marks. If Sally did well, she also scored high, unharmed by your own amazing performance.

When organizations become large or complex enough to require a formal approach to performance measurement, they nearly always select a rating system. These systems usually work for a while but eventually fall victim to the Lake Wobegon effect, with nearly all employees being jammed into the top two categories. Then someone at a high level snarls something like, "If you wimps can't make tough decisions, I will force you to"—and that's how most ranking systems are spawned. (The impetus for Jack Welch's famous "fire the bottom 10 percent" decree was his discovery that some poor performers at GE had been receiving bonuses and stock options.)

Ranking systems compare people not to expressed standards but to other people. Some ranking requirements are relatively benign. For example, teachers may be told to grade on a curve, with a maximum of 20 percent of their students receiving an A. Other ranking systems are severe, as when a manager is told to rank her engineers from one to twenty-four, with no ties. As mentioned, the purpose of most ranking systems is to force managers to make tough evaluation decisions, and since most managers comply, it works—but at a cost. First, ranking systems penalize managers who select or train their people exceptionally well. If you develop your people much better than I develop mine, your fourth-quartile employees may be better than those in my third quartile, but most ranking systems won't let you say so. Not only do ranking systems fail to exert pressure on managers with many low performers; in some cases the low performers become cherished assets. For example, if Bill and Leo have always been fourth-quartile performers and expect to be so labeled in the future, at review time they can be assigned their customary positions without a fuss, placing other team members safely on higher ground. (Among the strangest discussions you will ever have is when you tell someone on your team that his performance this year puts him, for the first time, in the bottom quartile and he asks, "What did I do wrong?" and you have to tell him, "Nothing, but Leo died.")

Another cost of ranking systems is that they discourage teamwork. When students are told they will be graded on a curve, they are less likely to form study teams. The business school at one of America's best universities typically hires several assistant professors each year and tells them, "In seven years, one of you may be granted tenure. Good luck!" These people do not coauthor publications or pursue research grants together, because accomplishments shared with a rival yield no competitive advantage.

Is this a bad thing? Not necessarily. In general, a good system is one that gets you what you want. If you want a culture of competition, a ranking system may be helpful. While at GE, I was asked by then vice chairman Larry Bossidy to devise a training program for his direct reports' businesses. When I met with each business leader to learn about his objectives and concerns, one of them—a brilliant man who ran one of GE's largest and most profitable businesses—asked, "You're not going to teach that collaboration crap, are you?" "Not now," I said, "but why do you ask?" He replied, "I've spent considerable time developing some friendly rivalries among my people, and maybe some not-so-friendly rivalries. Please don't screw up my culture."

Whether or not you share his belief that a competitive culture enhances performance, because he believed it, his use of a ranking system was appropriate. However, most executives want their culture to reflect teamwork and collaboration. Yet these executives often install, or permit their HR departments to install, quotas, quartiling, rank-and-yank systems, and other approaches that pit people against their colleagues.

To this point I have assigned the term "ranking" to any measurement process that compares people to other people. However, ranking systems differ in ways that have important implications for collaboration and employee development. Let's look at three of the most commonly used ranking systems—quartiling, bifurcation, and quotas:

- *Quartiling.* Quartiling violates two important measurement principles. First, it presumes that employee performance scores approximate a normal distribution. This is a risky assumption when a team is composed of fewer than thirty people, and most managers don't have thirty people directly reporting to them. Many firms try to solve this problem by combining people from different teams, but such people usually work on different things and report to different people, making comparisons unreliable. The second principle quartiling violates is this: never ask an evaluator to make distinctions in the middle of any array that even approaches a normal distribution, because there are always more objects in the center, causing the gaps between them to be narrower, which increases the capacity for measurement error. For example, try throwing thirty coins against a wall. A few will roll to the far right and a few to the far left, but most will bunch up toward the middle, with only small gaps between them. If you watch your managers quartile their people, you'll find that nobody starts in the middle. Most start by identifying their best person, then their second-best, then their third-best—continuing in this manner until, because they're getting closer to the center and the performance gaps are narrower, they hightail it to the other end of the distribution, where the distinctions between their worst performers, second-worst, and so on are clearer. If you had to rank, say, twenty people, wouldn't you do it the same way? Wouldn't you find it much easier to identify the top three and the bottom three than to distinguish between your ninth-, tenth-, and eleventh-best performers? And if you had to explain your rankings to a judge or a grievance committee, which rankings do you suppose would be most difficult to defend?

- *Bifurcating the workforce.* Here's an example of a ranking system that was initiated by a brilliant leader for the best of reasons, but because it violated the principles already examined, it created more problems than it solved. I mentioned earlier that Jack Welch was upset when he learned that some low performers at GE had received stock options. Consequently, Welch decreed that no more than half the people who had received stock options in both the two previous years could get them next time. (Jack said he would not permit the stock option program to "function like a dental plan"—i.e., be insensitive to performance.) What principles did this plan violate? First, Welch's edict put GE's employees in competition with one another. Second, it was unfair to GE's most productive employees, because, notwithstanding the awards to low performers that got Welch so upset, most of the repeat awardees were consistently high performers. Third, the plan required that evaluators differentiate between their fiftieth-percentile performers (who would get options next time) and those at the fifty-first percentile. (Had GE distributed options to the top 20 percent in year one and to the top 80 percent in year two, the percentage after year two would have approximated the 50 percent target Welch was seeking, but without causing people whose performance was virtually identical to be treated differently.)

- *Quotas.* Bifurcation and quartiling permit, but do not require, that the selection process be biased. Quotas, on the other hand, which Welch has called "substitutes for judgment and courage," ensure that decisions will be biased, with preassigned success and failure rates that are unrelated to the worth of individual candidates. For example, many organizations decide in advance that a specified, relatively high number of employees from some departments will be promoted, while other organizational units (e.g., "support," "the back office," or "the nonproducing divisions") are told they can promote almost no one. By predetermining in this way the number of winners, quota systems often stimulate intense competition, particularly within units whose promotion numbers are low. But probably the highest cost of quota systems is the diminution of individual self-esteem and unit pride that accompanies the painful reminder that senior management places such low value on the unit's contributions.

If quartiling, bifurcating, and quotas all have their drawbacks, is there an alternative that helps to resolve this rating versus ranking dilemma? Yes. In general, it is preferable for people to be assessed according to articulated standards, rather than being matched against their coworkers. While there is no substitute for standards that are tailored to fit your own organization's values and objectives, here are some universal criteria you can use to assess your employees' performance, regardless of their department, location, organization level, and occupational specialty.

Step 2

For performance assessment:

1. How good a job did the person do during the past year (or performance cycle)?

2. How important to the organization is the job that was done?

3. How difficult was it, given both internal and external conditions, to do a good job?

And for setting compensation:

4. How difficult would it be to replace the person in that job?

5. How does the person's compensation (and, for promotion purposes, organization level) compare to others inside and outside the organization?

6. Are there other factors (e.g., historical inequities, diversity considerations) to consider?

And for promotions:

7. How well does the person's performance in his or her present job predict likely performance in the new position?

These criteria permit an evaluator to take into account the same factors considered important by those who establish quotas. For example, if a computer technician and an investment banker perform their duties equally well, the banker could be paid more on the basis of question 2 and could be favored for promotion to senior banker on the basis of question 7. If a salesperson produces as much revenue in a poor territory as another salesperson generates in an affluent community, the former can be evaluated higher on the basis of question 3. Though both quotas and the seven-question rating approach permit consideration of the same factors and may often lead to the same promotion and compensation outcomes, the latter assesses each person's contributions on a case-by-case basis, rather than through an a priori stereotyping process that inadequately considers the performance of people as individuals.

True Versus Artificial Zero-Sum Games

Every organization faces tough decisions about goodies that are in short supply and crummy jobs that someone must do. Five people may believe they're next in line for the next promotion, window office, or conference in Bermuda. Conversely, business conditions may require that your nine-person office be reduced to seven or that someone on your staff needs to take a long, hard (and cold) look at why your Siberian operation isn't profitable. These are examples of true zero-sum games, in that one employee's gain is necessarily at others' expense. Of course, decisions like these require that employees be compared to one another, and nothing in this book is intended to suggest otherwise. If you need to fire 25 percent of your people, or promote 25 percent, or groom 25 percent for a special assignment, then quartiling may make good business sense. My arguments are intended to dissuade you from creating zero-sum games when there's no reason to. If managers in your organization are required to rank their people, you should make sure there's a good reason.

Let me close this discussion with perhaps the best known of all artificial zero-sum games: the selection process for the annual National Collegiate Athletic Association (NCAA) basketball tournament. The artificiality is caused by the unnecessary requirement that exactly sixty-five teams—no more, no less—are permitted to compete in this single-elimination tournament. Each year excellent teams are left out of the tournament, and each year their fans and the media lament their absence. And each year a representative of the selection committee goes before the television cameras to spout the same nonsense—that the choice was especially difficult this year because there were so many good teams and that so-and-so team could well have been selected, except that its "body of work" (I am not making this up) didn't quite measure up to that of the teams that were admitted. One such spokesperson recently summarized the selection committee's dilemma by saying, "Unfortunately, we had two gallons of water and a one-gallon tank."

Except that there isn't any one-gallon tank. This situation doesn't resemble in any way the dilemma of having one corner office and five people who want it. This situation arises because the committee is attempting to evaluate and then reward the performance of these teams without the benefit of prior definition. A far better approach would be to do what this book recommends. The NCAA (with input from the public, which would be marvelously entertaining) should specify what a team must do to get into the tournament. For example, perhaps a team should be required to win more games than it loses, overall and in its conference, and win at least three games against teams that are themselves tournament worthy, including at least one on the road. In other words, instead of predetermining the number of winners and permitting their worthiness to vary, why not hold the quality constant and let the "right" number of winners emerge? If, say, seventy-seven teams qualified one year, the lowest-ranking twenty-six would play a qualifying game (as teams ranked sixty-four and sixty-five do under the present system). If eighty-two teams qualified the next year, the lowest-ranking thirty-six would play an extra game, and so on. At the end of this qualifying round, sixty-four teams would remain, and the tournament could proceed as it does now.

I hope it's clear that this example is not particularly about basketball. It's meant to illustrate the dysfunctions that inevitably arise when an organization seeks to evaluate and reward performance without defining performance—transforming what could be an even-handed system that inspires people to excel against known standards into a system devoid of explicit criteria that must be defended by some poor soul staring into a TV camera and babbling like a lunatic about one-gallon tanks and two gallons of water. Even if you don't care about basketball, you should care that a similar approach to evaluation, causing the same dysfunctions, may be happening in your organization. For example, how does your organization handle promotions? Do you do what the NCAA does—predetermine the number of winners and losers and let the quality vary, so that those eligible in 2008 may have an easier path to promotion than those coming up a year later? If so, is it the result of a legal requirement (as is imposed on the U.S. Navy, whose maximum number of admirals is fixed by Congress)? If not, do you have a good reason for doing it?

If you don't have a good reason, why are you doing it?

Measuring the Right Things

Once you've identified what you're trying to achieve and have defined it in actionable terms, the next step is to see whether the behaviors you've identified are currently being measured. One way to do this is to take the output of the bull's-eye exercise—the list of behaviors you need more of or less of to accomplish your objective—and determine whether each item on the list is currently being measured. You must devise ways to measure those that aren't, because any behavior not measured can't be systematically rewarded, so there's an excellent chance it won't occur.

The Clean Sheet Exercise

Another way to ascertain that your goals and metrics are in alignment is to put your staff through the clean sheet exercise, named because of its premise: imagine that your organization has no metrics whatsoever—no budgets, no targets, nothing. Your secretary buzzes you and says, "You'd better take this call."

Who might it be? Your staff will easily name your important stakeholders: a customer, a regulator, a member of the board, a family member, someone from the media. They may also mention shareholders, suppliers, or the union. Then, taking the people named one by one, ask your staff to identify the dimensions on which you're vulnerable. For example, what might an angry customer say? Your staff will quickly identify the key elements of customer service: "You sent the wrong stuff"; "The shipment arrived late"; "It didn't arrive in working order"; "Your price is too high"; and so forth.

The object of the exercise is to answer two questions. First, if you had no metrics to start with, what would you have to keep track of to keep that telephone from ringing? If that's too rigorous a question, here's a gentler one: what would you have to monitor so that, when one of your important constituents calls with a problem, that phone call won't be the first time you hear about it?

Once your staff has answered these questions, have them put their responses on the left side of a flip chart, and on the right side, list all the things you measure now. Then search for anomalies in the two lists. There are two types. The more serious are the entries on the left that have no counterpart on the right. These identify your most important vulnerabilities—gaps in measurement such that the phone will have to ring before you know you have a problem. The rest of your meeting should be spent brainstorming how these can be measured. If you don't create lead indicators to prevent or, at least, give early warnings about these, you will be dependent on such lag indicators as returned products, complaint letters to the company president, negative morale surveys, exit interviews, and if you're especially unlucky, government indictments or the *60 Minutes* news team waiting in the lobby for you to arrive.

The opposite anomaly—entries on the right with no counterpart on the left—may mean you're measuring things no one cares about, but not necessarily. For example, in the course of doing the exercise, Johnson & Johnson executives identified a number of metrics, pertaining to various employee and community initiatives, that no one outside the company ever saw. This was not a defect. "We're committed to doing these things," they said during the debriefing. "It doesn't matter to us that the phone would never ring. That's not why we're doing it."

Objective Versus Subjective Metrics

Among the most cherished beliefs in the management literature concerns the existence of objective measures of performance. The belief is erroneous;

there is actually no such thing. (Consider the case of a museum guide who, when asked the age of a prehistoric carving, replies, "It's 1,000,004 years old." "What fantastic technology they have today," the inquiring visitor gushes; "how can they tell so precisely?" "Well," the guide replies, "they told me when I started that it was a million years old, and I've been here four years.")

If you think you have an objective metric, tell me what it is and give me a minute, and I'll show you how to look good on the measure while running your business into the ground. For example, would you like more cash? I'll show you how to depress your operating margins to get cash. Do you want inventory returns? You can sell off your stuff in December and then pay a 5 percent premium to buy it back in January.

Sales metrics. Sales is often portrayed as an exemplar of an objective, unambiguous performance metric. In a life insurance agency, for example, one can calculate policies sold, profit margins, and market share. However, such metrics will not reveal whether policies are being sold to dying people or to people who cannot afford to pay for what they have purchased, or whether service quality and customer goodwill are being maintained or systematically destroyed. Nor will these metrics shed light on whether senior salespeople are mentoring the younger staff and keeping the paperwork up to date. Similarly, in department stores, volume and profit on sales are always calculated, while directing business to other stores and enhancing the brand in the community are seldom measured. As another example, which do you consider to be the more important determinant of sales success: skill of the salesperson or fertility of the territory? Who will sell more—your best salesperson in, say, Peoria or a salesman with average skills whose territory is Scarsdale, Buckhead, or Beverly Hills? (If I seem a bit grumpy on this point, it's because I am. I once worked for an insurance company whose rewards included membership in the millionaire's club, composed of people who sold at least a million dollars of insurance within a specified period. Club members were treated to neat trips and cash prizes. The people I competed against did have the Scarsdale and Buckhead territories, as well as equally affluent routes in Grosse Point and Shaker Heights. I plied my trade in three- and four-story walk-ups in Maspeth, Queens, selling policies with $3-a-week and $10-a-month premiums. You do the math: how many millionaire club memberships do you figure I won?)

Financial metrics. Even the most formulaic measures of financial performance must be carefully interpreted. For example, if you own a ranch in New Mexico that cost you $90,000 in 1985 and earns $180,000 today, your return is 200 percent, which sounds pretty good—but the land is worth millions. Similarly, leasing an asset instead of buying it may be a poor use of funds from the firm's standpoint but will improve your return on assets. Return on equity is another performance measure that's easy to manipulate. As a final apocryphal example (from Norm Augustine, former CEO of Lockheed Martin): "The bright year-end profit picture was unfortunately diminished when it was discovered that of the $2 million reported earnings, $3 million had been derived from the sale of the research laboratory."

Sports metrics. The sports world offers many examples of supposedly objective metrics that actually require considerable interpretation. Runs batted in (RBIs), for example, is considered to be one of the most important statistics in baseball. It is used as the primary indicator of clutch performance, is part of baseball's triple crown, and correlates more strongly with compensation than any statistic other than seniority. However, when analyzed in conjunction with other operational measures, the only statistic a player's RBIs correlated with was the batting average of the person hitting ahead of him. (How's that for an equitable reward system? The better you do, the more I'm going to pay someone else next year.) What's needed, of course, is a comparison of a player's runs batted in with his opportunity to do so. Although "opportunity" would need to be subjectively defined, however defined, the resultant metric would be far more useful than RBIs is now.

I'd like to use another baseball example to illustrate the trade-off faced by nearly all executives: the desire to chronicle and highlight a subordinate's weaknesses (to establish a paper trail in case of future discipline, termination, or legal action) and the desire to intervene to correct, or at least mask, those weaknesses. Imagine that you are the manager of a National League baseball team, and one of your players is a great hitter but a horrible fielder. What do you do? First, put him in left field, where he can do the least damage. Second, get yourself a fast center fielder, station him in left center field, and tell him, "Go for everything; we've got nothing to lose." At season's end, who has more errors? Probably your center fielder, whose season is filled with diving catches and off-balance throws. You quite properly award him the larger bonus, only to be sued by your left fielder, who can prove "objectively" that he had a better year.

Two personal examples. While I was a dean at USC, I took part in many discussions about pay, promotion, and tenure. Seeking to make equitable decisions across departmental lines, my fellow administrators and I were always on the lookout for quantitative indexes that would make comparisons easier. We found, however, that even the most "objective" measures required subjective interpretation. For example, we gave a larger raise to a professor with two publications than to someone who, in our judgment, had published essentially the same paper four times. The second professor asked to meet with me, listened to the reasons behind my decision, and then said, "That's just your opinion!" My reply was, "You're right, but ultimately, that's what I have to rely on. And in my opinion, you didn't have a very good year."

Another example from my USC days pertains to a request by Gil Garcetti (who later became famous during the O. J. Simpson case) that I develop objective performance metrics for the lawyers in the Los Angeles County District Attorney's Office. I began the project as this book recommends—definition before measurement—but the senior leaders I interviewed defined performance in ways that could easily be gamed by the attorneys. A high percentage of convictions, for example, could induce prosecutors to shy away from difficult cases, and reduced trial time might lead to excessive plea bargaining. The final list of performance metrics ultimately proved useful but in no way eliminated the need for subjective assessment of how well each lawyer had performed.

Measuring What's Important

The common thread in all these examples is that it's important to measure what's important to measure. You don't get style points for easy, rigorous, or visible metrics. A bad formula is a poor substitute for good judgment.

No one sets out to base her measurement system on unimportant matters, yet many systems are built on just that. One reason is that the visible elements of performance tend to be overweighted, whereas the harder-to-see elements, though they may be of far greater importance, often don't get measured. Here are some examples:

- To improve customer service, many call centers have objectives concerning how many times a service representative's telephone should ring before it's answered. This aspect of customer service is important but gets more attention than is warranted. The metric reveals nothing about the quality of the interaction, the courtesy with which customers are treated, or whether their issues are satisfactorily resolved. Even though everyone knows these factors matter more to a customer than whether the phone is picked up after the third versus the fourth ring, they are often ignored because they are less visible.

- Sustained costs are usually visible; avoided costs (and benefits) are not, so often no one attempts to measure them. That's why, when smart people get together to spend the company's money, they so often make penny-wise, pound-foolish decisions. They often find, for example, that the small but easily identified costs associated with some new venture have been meticulously laid out for them, whereas the huge opportunity costs of not pursuing a project—the more subjective costs—have not been included. (In an attempt to counter this tendency, whenever I'm asked to defend the cost of a leadership development program, I offer this tautological reply: "The costs of leadership development are up front and calculable, and the benefits are down stream and intangible. If one of the firm's leaders ever makes a good decision as a result of the program, or avoids a bad one, that decision will pay for the entire program. Unless you think that won't happen, you should consider the program to be a good use of company funds.")

- Stories have been told for centuries about capsized sailors, near drowning, who were miraculously propelled toward shore by porpoises. This heartwarming image of the porpoise as a wet Good Samaritan has now been challenged by studies showing that porpoises really enjoy pushing things—any things, not just people, and in any direction, not just toward shore. Of course, the people who were pushed parallel to the coast or— even worse, farther out to sea—were less likely to be available later on to share their experiences.

Three More Measurement Dos and Don'ts

A variety of dysfunctional measurement practices are commonly employed in even the best-run organizations. Let's take a brief look at three of the most prevalent.

Measuring traits versus behaviors. Traits are relatively permanent. They do change over time, but not in response to an edict from the boss. They also cannot be observed directly so, unlike behaviors, are hard to measure. I have reviewed numerous performance appraisal forms during my career and have found that most of them seek to assess some combination of traits and behaviors. At GE, for example, we assessed a number of employee behaviors but also sought to measure energy, judgment, integrity, and creativity. (As noted earlier, these are "thought" and "emotion" words that go into the second ring in the bull's-eye exercise and need to be redirected to the center.) You should review the performance appraisal forms your firm has in place and, using the bull's-eye exercise or some other method, convert the descriptions of any traits you uncover into behaviors. Your reviews will be clearer and your recommendations more actionable, and you're less likely to be sued for telling someone he's a low performer.

Measuring performance versus promotability. In every organization there are people who are great at what they do, are poor candidates for promotion, and don't want to be promoted anyway. This is a wonderful state of affairs, and you shouldn't screw it up. What many firms do, however (and what we did at

GE until we realized our mistake), is to combine the performance and promotability scores into a single index. This has the effect of lowering the performance rating of people who are performing well but are unpromotable (which is unfair and, because it demotivates them, inefficient). It also causes these people to seek promotion (or at least, to seek to be promotable), which benefits no one. The right answer, obviously, is to keep the two dimensions separate.

Measuring performance quarter to quarter. The requirement that every American corporation must measure its performance every thirteen weeks—with the numbers then treated as meaningful, discrete data rather than merely one frame of a motion picture—results in a host of eccentric, unproductive behaviors. When I hear a CNBC reporter explain that such-and-such stock went down after a terrific quarter because people fear that the next quarter won't be as good, I visualize what it would be like if people applied this insane metric to other aspects of their lives. Imagine:

Dolores is upset.

Why?

She broke up with her boyfriend.

You're kidding! I thought they were doing so well.

They were. In fact, she said last weekend was the most romantic weekend of her life.

So why did they break up?

She knows that next time could never be as good. (She's also stopped going to that French restaurant because she had the best meal ever there, and she's not taking any more stock tips from her broker because the last tip tripled her money.)

Some Good News About Measurement

When you manufacture lightbulbs, you may have to break some of them to tell how well they're made. This technique, called "destructive testing," yields reliable data but leaves you with broken lightbulbs. The dilemma is solved by a process of random sampling, which may require that you test, say, only three lightbulbs from each batch of ten thousand. Your assembly-line workers know this and understood that the bulb they're working on at any moment has only one chance in 3,333 of being selected for testing. Yet they typically work hard to ensure that each bulb is well made.

Before I tell you what this shows, let me ask you two questions: (1) When you drive to work (or to the mall, or to visit friends), how many street corners do you pass? (2) On an average trip, how many police officers do you see? When I ask these questions in executive programs, the number of street corners is usually high and the number of police officers is always low, so I typically end up with a large ratio. For the sake of the example, let's assume that you travel five miles (so one hundred street corners) and typically encounter two police officers, for a ratio of fifty to one. I then ask: "If you come to a red light, do you usually stop?" (People always say yes.) "If we could afford to put a police officer at every corner, would compliance go up?" (Again, yes.)

What this shows is that a poor yardstick of performance is, usually, nearly as useful as a good one. If we had a police officer on every corner, compliance would go up but not by much, since most people obey the traffic laws anyway. Although the surveillance system in our example covers only one street in fifty, we're getting nearly the same results as we'd get from a system costing fifty times more. The ratio in our previous example was even more forbidding— only one lightbulb in 3,333—but the results were similar. However, if your community was to put up a sign that said, "Effective immediately, there will be no traffic surveillance of any kind between Fifth and Main streets," what would you get between Fifth and Main? Probably chaos. My point is, when you elect not to measure important aspects of performance (because those aspects are not visible, because they're hard to measure, or because your metric wouldn't be objective), you're effectively hanging a sign that says, "Effective immediately, there will be no surveillance of teamwork (or mentoring, or succession planning). You wouldn't do that between Fifth and Main. Why would you do it in your organization?

In most cases it's not the actual measurement that gives a system credibility; it's the capability for measurement. You don't have to measure each lightbulb or survey each street corner—you merely have to be able to. The person working on lightbulb 5,674 knows the odds are slim that that particular bulb will be sampled—but it could be. The quickest way to ruin the process is to tell people which three bulbs in the next batch will be tested. What you will get are three handcrafted, beautifully polished lightbulbs. What you won't get is useful information about the bulbs that aren't sampled. Similarly, in communities where the police's whereabouts are predictable, motorists slow down as they approach the speed traps and Dunkin' Donut shops and then speed up again afterward. The same thing occurs when the high school principal says to a teacher, "Next Tuesday I'm coming in to evaluate your class." What happens next Tuesday? More handcrafted lightbulbs.

The teacher is sober; he's borrowed notes from somebody. It's a pretty good class, but it reveals nothing about what happens the rest of the time.

As a final example, consider how the TV ratings organizations determine how many people are watching each television show. Not only are the networks told in advance which three time periods will be used to set advertising rates, but the same time periods are selected each year. Talk about handcrafted lightbulbs! Unpopular shows are taken off the air for a week or two and replaced by elaborate specials, major movie debuts, and titillating special features. Then, as if, say, 8 p.m. Wednesday on ABC has an intrinsic value that is independent of what show is on, advertising time is sold at rates that are based on these meaningless numbers. (Note that I am not faulting the networks, which are reacting rationally to the bizarre metrics that have been foisted on them.)

Measuring Everything That's Important

I said earlier that it's important to measure those things that are important to your organization's well-being. Now, supported by the examples in this section, I'd like to add a word to this advice and say this: it's important to measure (or at least, develop the capability to measure) *all* those things that are important to your organization's well-being. As noted earlier, many consultants recommend against setting a large number of objectives. They are concerned that too long of a list will cause people to lose focus, spend excessive time measuring, and fail to meet some of the many set goals.

I hope to dissuade you from this point of view by asking you to remember four things:

- The number of demands on your organization isn't up to you. You may prefer a small number, but if the demands are numerous, you're better off facing that fact or seeking a less complicated occupation than pretending that some of these demands don't exist. (A mirror in a messy room will reflect all the messiness, and it doesn't help matters to cover up part of the mirror; it's accurately capturing the phenomenon.)

- Once you have the ability to measure all your goals, you don't have to do so—at least, not often—so you won't spend all your time measuring. Furthermore, your sampling need not be random, so you won't lose focus. Many patrol cars are dispatched to direct traffic after a big game at the stadium, whereas the police department will seldom send a car to quiet suburban neighborhoods. But it could send a car, and once in a while it does. Similarly, you'll probably want to oversample the things you care most about while checking up occasionally on things that are less important.

- To be effective, your metrics need not be rigorous or sophisticated. Once you've operationally defined the things you care about, you'll find you can measure everything on your list. If at that point you're still having trouble with your metrics, you should consider using 360-degree appraisals, which are probably already in use somewhere in your organization. This technique enables you to gather performance data from peers, customers, suppliers, and others who will be impacted if the goal is accomplished. If none of these people can tell whether you've achieved your goal or are making progress toward it, then either you really haven't operationally defined it, or you should be asking yourself why you want it.

- Never underestimate the power of metrics to signal that something is important. I have visited organizations that talked endlessly about how much they valued team building, coaching, community involvement, succession planning, and candid feedback. Yet none of these things was incorporated into the annual performance reviews. Pressed to explain why such supposedly important aspects of performance weren't being measured, the leaders usually claimed that it wasn't because they didn't value those things but because it was so hard to measure them. Employees in these organizations—especially those who actually cared about these things—came to a different, more cynical conclusion.

In summary, don't worry that your list of objectives is too long; be afraid that it's too short. Don't forget a central premise of this book: if your definition of performance is incomplete, your metrics will be, too. And since things that aren't measured can't be rewarded, they very likely won't get done.

Anticustomer Metrics

Since nobody sets out to establish goals and metrics that harm customers, you have to wonder why it keeps happening. Here are some examples:

- Often, after someone from the GE travel bureau had booked my flight, he or she would say, "You have to call back to book your hotel." When I called back, I would usually get a different representative and had to go through the details all over again. I eventually learned that the reason the travel bureau was doing this was that it had installed a system that measured and rewarded employees based on the number of calls they handled.

- To induce service representatives to respond more rapidly to customer inquiries and complaints, some organizations have set objectives to reduce the interval between opening an e-mail and the customer rep's response. This metric contains two serious flaws. First, the reps soon realized that the clock didn't start until an e-mail was opened, so when they were busy, they stopped opening their customers' e-mails. Second, the metric would have been more customer-friendly if the word *action* had been substituted for *response*. Responses such as "we're looking into it" satisfied the definition, but usually not the customer.

- A well-known manufacturer developed goals and metrics that sought to improve the cycle time for goods coming from its factory. The metric was particularly sensitive to shipping delays at the end of the quarter. Unfortunately, the company defined "goods shipped" as those that were no longer on company property.

Not surprisingly, lots of product were shipped on March 31, June 30, and so forth. However, on the following morning, employees could hear banging coming from the direction of the parking lot. Looking up, they could see the product that had been "shipped," sitting on the railroad siding outside the plant and still being worked on.

- A particularly anticustomer metric that most readers are familiar with is one from the airline industry. Airlines label an "on time-departure" as any plane that leaves the gate within five minutes of its scheduled departure. You've probably enjoyed the experience of being squirreled away from the gate on time, only to sit for quite a while on the tarmac. There's more than one reason why this happens, but the metric governing on-time departures is no small contributor. (Does this example remind you of the previous one? It should. It's the same situation, only in this case, *you've* been shipped.)

Wing to Wing: A World-Class Customer-Friendly Metric

As a counterpoint to the previous examples, I'd like to share with you one of the most customer-friendly metrics I've ever seen. It became known as Wing to Wing because it began in GE's aircraft engine business, but the initiative soon took hold throughout the company. Derived from GE's Six Sigma program, Wing to Wing calls for employees to view the world through the eyes of their customers.

Here's an example of how it works. Large jet engines, such as those sold by GE, must periodically be sent to the service shop for maintenance, repairs, and replacement of parts. The engine might be off the wing for eleven days—seven days in the shop and four days coming and going. GE routinely set goals to reduce the time the engine was in the shop—say, from 7 days to 6.6 and then to 6.3, at which time GE would celebrate having trimmed fully 10 percent off the cycle time. Now, let's view the same event through the eyes of the customer. How long is the engine off the wing? Eleven days. Does the customer care that GE had possession of the engine for only seven of those days? No. From the customer's standpoint: (1) the engine is off the wing for eleven days; (2) it's a scientific fact that when the engine is off the wing, the plane cannot fly; (3) therefore, an expensive asset is sitting on the ground, incurring costs but no revenue; (4) and by the way, that 10 percent cycle time reduction GE is celebrating? It never happened.

Remember, the Wing to Wing philosophy requires that you see the world as your customer sees it. In the beginning this requires patience and a good pair of earplugs because there will be howls of protest from at least some of your employees. Wing to Wing strikes many people as unfair, because it violates the principle that you shouldn't hold people accountable for things that they can't control and that aren't part of their job. However, after they finished venting, GE's people began to be curious about the sources of delay during the four days the engine was out of their hands. They found a number of contributing factors, from union rules governing weekend work to IT problems that kept customers from realizing that their engines had been returned. A few factors turned out to be beyond GE's ability to remedy, but—thanks to the company's deep bench of Six Sigma–trained professionals—most were not.

Here's an example of Wing to Wing in action from GE Transportation, which supplies most of the world's locomotives. The business leader visited one of his good customers, the CEO of a railroad based in Texas, and told him that he was there to take a look at the world through the customer's eyes. The CEO replied, "Well, the first thing you need to understand is that we keep things simple down here. We label days as 'good days' and 'bad days.' And since you asked, it does piss us off a bit that you sometimes act like you're having a good day when we're definitely having a bad day." Although the business leader's own dashboards were much more sophisticated, he decided that if that's how his customer saw the world, then so would GE Transportation. What happened next? The customer managed to crash two GE locomotives together at a siding. No one was hurt, but the engines were severely damaged. Before Wing to Wing, GE's employees might have regaled one another for days with the saga of the customer who threw the wrong switch and destroyed two engines. Instead, they concluded that even though the engines had not malfunctioned, GE had had a bad day, because the customer had. Several black belts—certified Six Sigma experts—were dispatched to Texas to determine why it happened and make sure it wouldn't happen again. These visits to customers became the basis for a separate initiative, called "at the customer, for the customer," that permitted GE to obtain useful market intelligence while adding tremendous value to its customers.

A final example of using Wing to Wing to improve a customer's core processes comes from another GE business, Fleet Services. This is how the process worked before and after its adoption, as described by one of GE's black belts:

> We created nineteen distinct vehicle configurations. Then the customer prepared eight hundred order packets and mailed them to the drivers. The customer then followed up and monitored responses, and handled an average of four hundred calls—questions from the drivers or calls to the drivers regarding bad information they had submitted. Then there was a six- to eight-week wait to receive the car. We reduced our part from three to four days to two minutes with online solutions. But from the customer's standpoint, this change had no impact on the total process. Working on the customer's internal process, and giving them a Six Sigma online solution, reduced the process significantly and eliminated 40 percent of the driver calls and cut the cost of remaining calls way down.

If this idea is a new one for your organization and you'd like to take a first step toward viewing the world through your customer's eyes, ask your customer representatives, "Do you know what makes your customer a hero or a bum in his or her organization?" Don't settle for general responses such as "increased revenue" and "reduced costs." Drill down. Does your rep know how and when revenue is booked in his client's organization? Does he know whether his client's firm considers earnings or operating margin to be of greater importance? Does he know whether his client is under pressure to generate high returns or whether preserving capital is considered more important? If your people can't answer such questions, ask them to schedule a meeting with their best clients to find out.

Step 3: Create Reward Systems That Work

Let me begin this section by asking you two questions:

- In a typical organization, who gets more money—high performers or low performers? (Most people say the high performers.)

- In a typical organization, who gets more performance feedback—high performers or low performers? (Most people say the low performers.)

According to the dictionary, rewards are anything that increases the probability of a future response. Viewed that way, money is obviously a good reward. If you offer people money to do something, you increase the likelihood that they'll do it. Feedback is also a good reward. In the absence of feedback, it's impossible for people to systematically improve their behavior. Now, if I told you there's a firm in town that systematically gives the highest pay to the low performers, you'd say that its leaders must be crazy. Yet the majority of organizations give most of their performance feedback to the low performers. Why does this occur? In large part because managers typically don't think of feedback as being a reward. In many firms, rewards are almost entirely about money.

Does your organization think of rewards that way? One warning sign is if your people use the term *reward and recognition system* to describe the incentives you offer. If so, you should ban that term, because it implies that rewards mean money, and recognition is that cute, touchy-feely other stuff you're supposed to do. *Financial and nonfinancial rewards* is a superior term to convey the message that some of the most powerful rewards do not involve the distribution of money.

Rewarding Things Right

Maybe you have the right metrics in place and you're measuring the right things. Maybe you have even considered how your organization talks about rewards. If so, you're a step ahead of most companies. But before we can delve into the next subject—rewarding the right things—let's look at how most firms reward employees now, starting with a more in-depth review of financial rewards and moving on to prestige rewards and content rewards.

Financial Rewards

One reason money is a good reward is that no one refuses it, no one returns it, and most people will go to great lengths to get more. Offering too much of other rewards can be as unattractive as too little. Excessive responsibility can cause an ulcer, for example, and too much freedom can lead to role ambiguity and confusion, but even huge amounts of money are accepted without complaint. The use of money as a reward, however, also has significant limitations, the most obvious of which is that it's seldom available in sufficient quantities to attract, motivate, and retain all those who are deserving.

Money is problematic even when it is available, because it's the ultimate commodity. If people stay with you because of the money, they will leave when someone offers more. This is especially true of your high performers, who are often worth more to another firm than to you. For example, there are perhaps five hundred people in Goldman Sachs who have deep knowledge of the firm's systems and processes. At XYZ Co., which is not as well managed, only a handful of people really know how Goldman operates. If XYZ wants to increase that number—for self-improvement or to be more competitive with Goldman—the value to XYZ of a few good Goldman Sachs employees exceeds what they are worth to Goldman, so XYZ will offer to pay them more.

A final shortcoming of financial rewards is that they are tricky to administer. When distributed intelligently in pursuit of organizational goals, money is a good investment. When dispensed foolishly, the money is still gone (since nobody returns it), but you haven't purchased motivation, productivity, or anything else of value. You haven't made an investment; you've merely increased your cost of doing business. Do organizations, even well-managed organizations, distribute money foolishly? Yes. Financial rewards in most firms tend to fail many of the tests of a good reward system. (This point will be elaborated on shortly.)

Prestige Rewards

These rewards sometimes cost money to administer and, by elevating the status of those who receive them, can improve one's future earning power. However, their intention is not to benefit employees financially but to increase the stature of employees in the eyes of colleagues and others. Frequently used prestige rewards include job titles; access to executive clubs and dining rooms; office size, location, and furnishings; and the right to fly first-class or use the company plane.

Job Content Rewards

The third and final category of rewards is job content rewards. The renowned psychologist Frederick Herzberg once remarked, "If you want your people to do a good job, give them a good job to do." Performance feedback, mentioned earlier, is one of a number of attributes that can serve as important content rewards but are often not thought of as rewards and so are underutilized. Other rewards based on job content include responsibility, challenge, recognition, autonomy, and opportunities to participate in decision making, to grow professionally, and to do interesting and important work. Common examples of rewards of this type include acknowledging someone for work well done, asking people's opinions about changes that will affect them, and telling a subordinate that you trust her to complete an important job on her own. As another example, scientists in many research labs used to be required to write papers and apply for patents in their employers' name. Then it was determined that the company's legal rights were in no way jeopardized by permitting the scientists to put their names on their work. This proved to be an important content reward that cost the company nothing.

Two additional examples of content rewards come from my experience at Goldman Sachs.

Soon after joining the firm I was asked to brief an important committee about the executive coaching program. The program was part of Pine Street (Goldman's leadership development unit, which I headed), but it was in place when I arrived, very capably run by Cary Friedman, one of the firm's associates. "Fine," I said. "Cary and I will be there." "You don't understand," I was told, "You're supposed to come alone. The most senior person always presents. Cary can brief you beforehand." I replied that I wasn't about to go without Cary—because the committee would get better information from him than from me, and because he had done all the work and was entitled to be there. The first question I was asked in the briefing was how many of my coaches are academics and how many are consultants. I had no idea, but Cary knew the answer to that and every other question I was asked. After that day, whenever committee members had questions about the program, they called Cary directly—good information for them, and great exposure for him.

Not long afterward, President and Co-COO John Thornton called me to his office to tell me how happy he was with some of the Pine Street initiatives. As I listened I realized that, unfortunately for me, none of the things I was being complimented for were of my doing. They had all been conceived, and were being implemented, by members of the Pine Street team. I said, "John, excuse me, but I'm feeling funny about this meeting, because you're congratulating the wrong person. We have ten minutes left of the scheduled time. Can I come back with my team so they can hear these things from you directly?" John agreed, so my team and I came back a few days later, and the ten minutes John had scheduled to talk to team members stretched to fifty, as he, in great detail, elaborated on how our team was adding value, what tasks remained to be done, and how Pine Street could play a major role in the transformation of the culture of Goldman Sachs if we were willing to take some risks and put in the effort. You can imagine the effect on the Pine Street team, who were mostly junior people, of being invited to the thirtieth floor and given detailed feedback and a call to action by one of Goldman's most senior people.

I said earlier that one of the drawbacks of financial rewards is their occasional unavailability. This is also true of prestige rewards, which, to be prestigious, must be somewhat scarce. (If you worked in a building with an arboretum in the center, every employee could have a window office, so it would not be prestigious to have one.) On the other hand, one of the most important advantages of content rewards lies in their availability. Such things as challenge, recognition, interesting work, and job autonomy are never mentioned in the contract, or the budget, or the union agreement; you literally create your own supply. For example, you can give feedback to someone and then give it to someone else. You can give your employees opportunities to participate in decision making today and then give them additional opportunities tomorrow; you're limited only by your imagination. Ironically, because we're so attached to the idea that value comes from scarcity, this attractive feature of content rewards—their unlimited availability—may be why so many managers underutilize them. If you told your managers they could give performance feedback to no more than three people in the next six months, they might begin to think seriously about how to use this suddenly scarce resource. But because there's no limitation, some of them are probably not even using their quota of three.

Tests of a Good Reward System

I said earlier in this section that financial rewards are typically distributed in ways that fail many of the tests of a good reward system. Now I want to identify those tests, but before I do, I'd like you to (1) think of a reward in your organization that you believe is working well, and (2) think of one that's not working well. Later in this section, I'll make some guesses about the two rewards you've named.

Availability and eligibility. Rewards may be unavailable for a variety of reasons that are nobody's fault. Ineligibility, on the other hand, is nothing less than intentional unavailability. Most organizations make certain rewards available only to specific categories of people—managers but not individual contributors, for example, or managing directors but not vice presidents. The purpose of such practices is often to motivate people to climb the organizational ladder. Rewards commonly used for this purpose include stock grants and options, profit sharing, deferred compensation, and invitations to participate in attractive investment opportunities. Equally motivating to employees at lower levels is the desire to escape jobs with poor job content. Thus, residents and interns work impossibly long hours to become MDs; newly minted lawyers, accountants, and consultants toil mightily to become partners; and assistant professors strive for promotion and tenure.

Unfortunately, this conception of rewards and careers became popular long ago, when bigger meant better and managers were rewarded for adding layers, staff, and budget. Today, inducing large numbers of employees to lust after the top-level jobs is counterproductive. Following the wave of delayering and downsizing of the 1990s and the financial instabilities since then, today's most productive companies have fewer organizational levels and high-level positions. Consequently, today's best-run firms are increasingly seeking to weaken the relationship between organizational rewards and hierarchical advancement so as to permit employees to have a good career without necessarily ascending to the top of the hierarchy. Thus, many firms have expanded their eligibility criteria for stock options; have gone from narrow- to wide-banding (making it possible to meaningfully increase people's salaries without promoting them); and have experimented with skill- and knowledge-based pay, dual ladders, and horizontally focused careers, whereby employees can advance into increasingly influential positions without moving upward.

Two additional dysfunctions of ineligibility are worth mentioning. First, when you place people in different categories (e.g., hourly vs. salaried, full-time vs. contract worker, manager vs. supervisor), you give them different points of view. In today's increasingly diverse organizations, it's hard enough to rally employees around common values and priorities without creating additional distinctions. Second, when you make people ineligible for a reward, you take away their motivation to strive for it. For example, the odds in most U.S. state lotteries are so bad that you're more likely to be killed on your way to buy a ticket than you are to win first prize, yet millions of people buy tickets. Now suppose your state decides that, to save money, no one whose last name begins with M is eligible to win. If your name starts with an M, will you buy a ticket? Of course you won't, but why not? They haven't substantially reduced your chances. The odds against your winning were millions to one before the decision and are virtually the same (i.e., zero) afterward. Psychologically, however, it makes a huge differences to know that, no matter how lucky or deserving you are, you will not be permitted to win.

This practice of making employees ineligible for various rewards is often so deeply ingrained that people are scarcely aware that they're doing it. Here's an example: while visiting a Goldman Sachs client in London, I was asked to critique an exciting but controversial new bonus plan the company was about to unveil. I asked my host, "What makes it controversial?" He explained that the plan called for including only a handful of executives, but he and a few others were arguing to include additional employees. I asked what percentage of all employees would be covered under each version of the plan. He replied that the plan covered 2 percent of employees, but the version he favored would add another 7 percent. He asked what I thought. I said, "Let me see if I've got this straight. You've designed this exciting plan that you believe will retain top talent and motivate people to be more productive. You've already decided to exclude 91 percent of your people, and now you're fussing over how many of the remaining 9 percent to disqualify."

Here's another example: I was engaged by a client to teach a course on performance reviews and asked who the participants would be. He replied that the course would be offered to all the managing directors (MDs)—unless I had a better idea. I replied, "Why not offer the course to all the firm's blue-eyed people?" He understood my point, which was that the firm's managing directors had little in common beyond their titles. (Some of these MDs led large organizations, while others were individual contributors with no one to review.) I then asked whether people below the MD level did performance reviews (they did) and whether the firm offered other courses to help those people (it didn't). So I asked, "Why don't we offer the course to everyone who wants to get better at giving performance reviews?" My point in relating these stories is not to pretend that I'm smarter than my clients but to illustrate how the concept of ineligibility can become so deeply rooted in an organization's culture that it becomes automatic and unconscious.

Now, I understand that sometimes there isn't enough money to go around and that legal or cultural reasons may dictate that certain classes of employees be treated differently. The tests presented here—availability, eligibility, and the ones to be introduced shortly—aren't immutable laws to be followed blindly. They are, however, supported by a good deal of research, theory, and common sense, so they shouldn't be dismissed out of hand. If your rewards are failing any of these tests, you should make sure there's a good reason why. When the head of GE Plastics couldn't find a good reason for the prevailing practice of inviting employees to the annual off-site solely on the basis of organizational level, the invitation list was expanded to include the year's top performers, regardless of level. That year, a few individual contributors were invited. This added almost nothing to the cost of the meeting, but it honored and motivated the junior people who were selected and signaled to everyone in the company that performance, not just titles, was what mattered at GE Plastics. Remember, your low-level people don't have large budgets and platforms to accomplish great things, so you don't have to worry about hordes of junior people storming your off-site. You don't have to post a sign that says, "Only officers are welcome" to prevent it from getting out of hand. Just make sure your performance criteria are rigorous. Then, once in a while, someone far down in your organization will accomplish something so significant that you'll want to honor her contribution at the annual meeting. The prospect of this happening should excite you. It doesn't matter how often it occurs; the point is that you should have a process that permits it to occur.

However, if you do decide to make your rewards more inclusive, don't lose sight of a central premise of this book: increasing eligibility will make your rewards more powerful but, by doing so, will put more pressure on your metrics. Inviting three low-level employees to your annual off-site may cause three thousand people to wonder why they weren't invited, too. That's why it's critical to make sure your metrics are competent before you increase the power of your rewards.

This caveat segues nicely into our final example of ineligibility: CEO compensation. When one person receives hundreds of times more money than others in the same company, it's essential that metrics exist to defend the disparity. If the firm has not performed well, the two main arguments in favor of compensating the CEO so generously—that he has earned the money, so the reward is equitable, and that the payout is necessary to retain him, so the reward is efficient—lose their credibility. It then becomes obvious that the CEO has received the reward because of title, not performance. In other words, the leader has been given a reward for which everyone else is ineligible.

Visibility. To be effective, at a minimum, rewards must be visible to those who receive them. Some rewards fail this test. For example, a Detroit firm found that good people were leaving for what the firm calculated to be inferior offers. Exit interviews revealed that, because the firm's generous benefits program was described in such actuarial double-talk, people were underappreciating its value. The solution was to create a cartoon booklet that enabled employees to comprehend what their benefits were worth. As another example, I once was enrolled in a benefits program where the premiums were paid by my employer. Since the organization's contribution was invisible, most employees took it for granted. The problem was easily solved by printing the employer benefit payments on the pay stubs.

To be maximally powerful, rewards should be visible not only to recipients but also to others. If you reward someone for a good job by giving her a thousand-dollar bonus, the number of people you've motivated is either one (if she's pleased) or zero (if she thinks she should have received more). This is not an effective use of company funds. Consider two of the world's most attractive rewards: the Nobel Prize and the Academy Awards. If the rules required that the ceremonies be private and the winners' names anonymous, would people still want to win? Of course, but the awards wouldn't mean nearly as much.

Of all the tests of a good reward, visibility is the one most often violated. This violation is intentional, especially with financial rewards; most organizations offer no more visibility than is legally required. Many public sector organizations make their financial arrangements public, and corporations provide compensation information about their most senior people—but only because they have to. Ironically, a number of studies have shown that when financial rewards are not disclosed, most employees believe they are worse off, relative to their fellow workers, than is actually the case. If financial rewards were made public, the dominant reaction might well be one of relief.

By making your rewards more visible, you will increase their power, which will again test the credibility of your metrics. In cases where the metrics can withstand the scrutiny, rewards are sometimes made visible even when there is no legal requirement to do so. Consider the contests held in many companies, with the winners offered a weekend for two to Bermuda or Hawaii. If you have such contests, for whom do you have them? Probably your salespeople. Do you make the award, and the winner's name, visible? Definitely. Why do you run contests for your salespeople but not for your technicians? Because you believe you have good, objective sales data (though actually you don't, as was noted previously) that justifies the awards. If your technicians' performance metrics were sufficiently credible, you could make their rewards visible as well.

The reluctance to making financial rewards visible is deeply rooted in most organizations' cultures and is unlikely to be overcome by anything written here. However, increasing the visibility of the nonfinancial rewards is usually a much easier sell, and there are great gains to be had by doing so. Many actions that require little or no financial outlay—inviting a team to present its proposal to senior management, for example, or recognizing someone for assisting another division—are usually much more powerful if made public. Be careful, however, not to reward someone publicly if doing so will get him in trouble with his peers. When I worked at GE, a progressive labor leader took several actions that benefited union members and were also very helpful to division management. On one of his visits to the business, Jack Welch went out onto the shop floor and, after talking briefly with the union leader, started to give him an appreciative hug. The leader backpedaled as if Welch was contagious. Later, he told GE's CEO, "If you want to hug me in private, that's fine. But all I need is for someone to take a picture, and I'm dead in the next election."

Performance contingency. While other factors play a role, rewards should be based more on performance than on seniority, titles, or organizational membership. Much more will be said about this later.

Timeliness. To be maximally effective, rewards should be received soon after the reward-worthy action has occurred. If a rat in a cage pulls a lever and six months later (on his anniversary date) a lump of sugar falls down, he will not link the reward with the action. Although people track better than rats, employees who are required to wait a long time for a reward are likely to conclude that when it's due to arrive, they won't still be there, or the boss won't be there, or the reward won't be there, or they'll screw up in the meantime and no one will remember what a good job they did. Even when receipt of the reward is certain, the longer the interval, the less the recipient will see its connection to performance. For an example of how timeliness adds power, compare these two scenarios: (1) At the annual performance review, Jane's boss tells her, "One thing that has impressed me is your comments at the leadership council meetings. You really keep people on track and help focus the discussions." (2) Ten minutes after the conclusion of a leadership council meeting, Jane's boss drops by her office and says, "I just want to say thank you for your comments today. They really helped everybody get back on track and focused the discussion." Same boss, same message—but won't the feedback in the second scenario have a much greater impact on Jane?

Organizations extend the interval between performance and rewards in a number of ways. Sometimes procedures require so many sign-offs and layers of review that by the time the reward is approved, it's hard to remember what it's for. (In the early days of GE's Work-Out program, a contest developed among the consultants about who could uncover the longest string of required approvals before a reward could be dispensed. I came upon a reward that required six sign-offs but lost to someone who found one that required nine.) Also contributing to delays are policies that delay disbursement of the reward until the employee's anniversary date or until the end of the calendar or fiscal year. Such policies sometimes serve a purpose, but often they are merely legacies from the days when data were stored on punch cards and fed in large batches into giant mainframe computers. Today's technology does not require that data be aggregated, making it possible to more closely link rewards with the actions being rewarded.

Sometimes there are good reasons for the delay. Universities reward faculty for publications, but books and journal articles are often not accepted for publication until long after they're written. Corporations encounter the same difficulty with respect to copyrights and patents. As another example, Goldman Sachs ties employee compensation to the firm's revenues, which aren't known until the end of the fiscal year. In such cases, however, the organization can still make some general comments about the timetable of the reward and the criteria on which it will be based. This lacks the motivational punch of immediacy but is much better than saying nothing.

Reversibility. One of the annoying attributes of being human is that anytime you make a decision, there's a decent chance it's a bad one. (If you're at a high level and that isn't true of you—if your decisions always work out well—you're probably doing stuff you should be delegating.) Consequently, a nice property of any decision is reversibility—the ability to undo an outcome you don't like or, at least, cut your losses and prevent its repetition. In terms of reward systems, reversibility can be defined two ways. Ideally, it means being able to take back a reward you shouldn't have given—perhaps reclaiming someone's company car, stripping him of his title, or taking him out of the partnership. However, it's often impossible to take back a reward after it's distributed, so the less rigorous definition of reversibility is that the decision to dispense the reward can be reversed and the recipient won't automatically get it again. Some rewards are, for all practical purposes, irreversible. For example, though procedures may exist to reclaim an employee's base pay, the appeals processes and paperwork are sufficient to discourage anyone who's not a masochist from making the effort. Therefore, erroneously increasing someone's salary effectively creates an annuity over his organizational lifetime, and since future raises are typically influenced by base salary, your error will become increasingly expensive over time. That's why reversible compensation by any name—bonuses, incentive pay, variable compensation, compensation at risk—is an attractive vehicle for distributing financial rewards. Because there's no obligation to make payments in future years unless performance remains high, such rewards pass the performance contingency test and are also reversible. Reversible compensation can also serve as a shock absorber, by permitting an organization to reduce payroll without taking out people.

The greatest difficulty with reversible rewards is their tendency to become calcified over time. The interval between giving employees a gift or a bonus and their perception of it as an entitlement has been found to be an hour and a half (or so it seems). Many corporations have had to jettison their bonus plans because the payouts came to be so taken for granted that the incentive component became just another name for base pay. In one well-publicized case, senior management thanked employees for an excellent year by giving each of them a holiday turkey. A year later management did the same thing, but when year three wasn't as profitable, management withheld the turkey and then had to withstand a storm of complaints and criticisms from irate employees who had been denied their "traditional" holiday turkey. During the twenty-four months between year one and year three, the turkey had somehow morphed from a generous gift into an irreversible commitment on the part of the company.

What can you do about this? There are no quick fixes, but here are a few tips:

- If you give people a turkey this year, give them something else—anything else—next year.

- If you give people a gift in December this year, give it in some other month next year.

- If you distribute the gift in the office this year, mail it to their homes next year.

In short, for a reward to remain reversible, it has to look and feel reversible. If you don't vary your routine from the start, you may not be able to later.

Advantages of Job Content Rewards

I noted earlier that financial rewards are often unavailable and prestige rewards are necessarily so, but content rewards are limited only by your desire to use them. I hope to convince you now that content rewards perform exceptionally well against all the tests of a good reward system:

- *Eligibility.* Since ineligibility is nothing more than intentional unavailability, the restrictions on money and prestige we've already noted apply here. On the other hand, feedback, recognition, opportunities to participate, and the other content rewards we've identified are seldom subject to eligibility requirements.

- *Visibility.* As previously mentioned, most financial rewards are not visible. Prestige rewards must be visible, at least to some people, since it can't be prestigious to have something if no one knows you have it. Content rewards can be as visible as you wish to make them.

- *Performance contingency.* In general, all three reward types have the potential to pass this test. However, some of the most costly financial rewards—retirement benefits, for example, and life and health insurance—are only indirectly related, if at all, to performance. The same is true of many prestige rewards—for example, invitations to off-sites and twenty-year service awards. On the other hand, such content rewards as job autonomy, recognition, and opportunities to participate in decision making are usually performance based.

- *Timeliness.* As previously mentioned, there are often long delays between performance and financial rewards. Prestige rewards, too, must sometimes be put off (e.g., waiting until the award ceremony to receive a medal or waiting for a window office to become available). Content rewards, on the other hand, can usually be administered quickly.

- *Reversibility.* As noted earlier, some financial rewards are reversible, but many are not. Prestige rewards, too, are often hard to undo. (Have you ever tried to persuade someone to vacate his window office?) Content rewards, however, are usually reversible. If you gave someone more job freedom, for example, and you haven't seen her since then, you can take it back. If you gave someone more challenge or responsibility than he can handle, you can fix it. Since they're reversible, errors pertaining to your content rewards are less costly, so you can be innovative and take greater risks.

These advantages are not just textbook theory; real-world examples are plentiful. For example, what do rehabilitation counselors, primary school teachers, soldiers, nuns, charity workers, and registered nurses have in common? Their pay is low and their prestige is ordinary, but their job content tends to be high and often generates unusually high levels of motivation and morale.

Evaluating the Rewards Your Organization Is Using

Earlier in this section I asked you to identify a reward that's working well in your organization and one that isn't. Now I'd like to make three guesses about what you've written:

- The reward that's working well passes all, or nearly all, the tests of a good reward system.

- The reward that's not working well is failing at least a couple of the tests.

- The reward that's working well costs your organization no more than the reward that's working poorly.

My third assertion is based on responses I've received from numerous organizations, which cause me to conclude that the best rewards are better because they pass the tests, not because they cost more. Of course, your individual response may be different, but if you ask your people these questions, I predict that their overall responses will demonstrate that the power of a reward is unrelated to its cost. The key to improving the effectiveness of your reward system is to administer your rewards in such a way that it passes the tests.

Evaluating Some Rewards Other Organizations Are Using

Just for practice, let's take a look at some rewards through the lens of the tests we've been discussing to see how they stack up.

First is an example from the banking industry. One of the largest U.S. banks distributed play money to all its employees, instructing them to award it to the colleague outside their work group who had best helped them achieve their work objectives. Recipients could redeem the play money for real cash. This program passed all the tests we've identified and was judged by the bank to be very successful. Another, and always desirable, feature of the reward is that it contained elements of money, prestige, and job content.

Another reward wasn't as successful. When I taught in executive programs at the University of Michigan, I would ask students whether anyone in their organization had told them why they were selected to participate and, if so, what they had been told. Twenty-five percent had been told only where and when to show up. Of the 75 percent who were told something, most of the explanations were positive (e.g., "You did a great job on your last project, and we're thinking of a bigger role for you"). Some participants were given a neutral rationale (e.g., "The firm sends someone each year, and this year that person is from our division"), but others were told that the course was remedial (e.g., "You need private coaching, but this is cheaper") or were given the impression that they were selected because the really productive people couldn't be gone for two weeks. The cost of the program was the same for all attendees, but by making the participant feel good about being selected, and by making the designation performance contingent and timely, some companies converted the cost into an investment, while others did not. I also asked attendees, "If you learn something useful, do you have a forum back home to share what you've learned?" Most didn't, but the best firms did. Establishing a setting for participants to let their fellow employees know what they've learned and what changes they recommend does the following: (1) it causes participants to be fully engaged in the program; (2) it provides them with visibility and recognition when they return home; (3) it gets other employees enthused about attending executive programs; and (4) it greatly increases the value of what's been learned to the firm. The back-home forum need not be elaborate. Some organizations set a time during senior committee meetings when executives just back from executive programs make brief presentations. In other firms the forum is an open house after work or a lunchtime get-together.

The executive program example was a missed opportunity for most of the companies sending employees, but the results could have been worse. They could have been disastrous. Consider the large corporation that invited seventy-five people each year to a lavish dinner cruise, hosted by the CEO and other senior executives. Those selected were designated by the company as "the people who make a difference." The selection criteria were not well known. What was well known is that the same people, all of them high-level employees, were selected every year. (How do you like it so far?) One year, on the evening of the cruise, some of the perennially rejected employees threw an office party for "the people who don't make a difference," got satisfyingly drunk, and took out their frustrations on the fixtures and furniture. It's possible that those who were invited earned the reward each year, but in the absence of known criteria, most people who weren't invited concluded that it wasn't performance contingent, that you had to be at a high level to be invited (ineligibility), and that once you were invited to one cruise you were invited to all of them (irreversibility). The fact that the reward was so visible added to its power, but in the absence off credible metrics, making it visible did more harm than good.

And the examples of what not to do with employee rewards continue. Earlier in this section I spoke about a Detroit organization that spent a great deal of money on a showcase benefits plan that most employees didn't understand and, as a result, didn't appreciate. This same company, in a minor cost-cutting initiative, halted its financial support for some employee after-hour activities, including its Canadian division's hockey team—in the middle of the season! This nearly resulted in a wildcat strike. In another case a large office supply retailer had, for years, been rewarding the employees who exceeded their quotas with pizza parties on Friday evenings after the store closed. Eventually, someone in the home office thought to ask the employees what they felt about the parties and was told, in no uncertain terms, "We would prefer cash bonuses, rather than pizza with people we spend the entire week with." (The moral of these stories is, know your people well enough to be able to predict which rewards they do, and don't, find attractive.)

How do you avoid the horror stories and follow in the path of, say, that U.S. bank and its successful reward program? I believe that the recommendations made so far will enhance your ability to define, measure, and reward performance. These recommendations are necessary, but are not sufficient, to ensure that you will be successful. The more closely you follow them, the more powerful will be your reward system and the greater will be its capacity to help you—or hurt you. What remains is to make certain that you are rewarding the right things—that is, the things you want your people to do.

Rewarding the Right Things

Perhaps the closest thing to a universal truth about motivation is that people pursue pleasure—though we don't all find the same things pleasurable—and seek to avoid pain. Consequently, people join work organizations for personal, "selfish" reasons, hoping that through membership and participation in organizational activities at least some of their needs will be satisfied. Because people are so different, employees are unlikely to pursue with equal passion any particular organizational goal or mission. This divergence of personal needs is a constraint, but not necessarily a critical one, on an organization's ability to achieve collective outcomes. A key factor is whether the organization's reward systems encourage or discourage its members from pursuing these outcomes. This problem is often identified as one of motivation, but it's really a matter of goal alignment. Employees who regularly call in sick on Monday, sneak out to get coffee, or go home at night with half your firm's office supplies in their briefcase are engaging in highly motivated behavior. You just don't like it!

Since these actions are not aligned with the organization's goals, organizations try to prevent them from occurring. The first attempt to do this is through selection, trying to keep the "wrong" people from becoming members, but inevitably, some misfits are admitted. The next tool in the kit is orientation and training, through which employees are exposed to, and hopefully embrace, the organization's norms and traditions. Unfortunately, such training tools are far better suited to improve people's skills and knowledge than to alter their needs and values. Therefore, the third tool to achieve employee-organization alignment in cases where selection and training are not wholly successful is the definition-measurement-reward process that has been the primary focus of this book. Rather than regarding "selfishness" as a lamentable flaw in the human condition, effective reward systems induce organization members to pursue organizational goals for that most reliable of reasons: each person's conviction that he or she will benefit by doing so.

Reward System Trade-offs

I noted earlier that a sine qua non of any good reward system is that it gets you what you want. Knowing what you want may not sound complicated, but unfortunately, often the things you want are inextricably accompanied by other things that you don't much care for. Therefore, even if your reward system has been well assembled, you sometimes have to make difficult choices. Let's now take a look at four important reward system trade-offs that have not yet been discussed but are key factors to consider as you endeavor to reward the right things.

Trade-off 1: Rewarding efficiency versus equity. Efficiency has both subjective and objective elements, but equity is almost entirely subjective and is strongly influenced by cultural forces. In many countries equity means saying thank you for work previously done. This is sometimes referred to as "pay for (past) performance." In some societies it means paying everyone nearly the same. For example, many Danish employees are opposed to bonuses and pay raises that are a percentage of salary, because they want everyone to receive the same increase. In other cultures equity means paying for the length of service or giving more money to people who need more money, as when Japanese firms increase people's pay when they marry or have a child. (That's also why some Japanese firms pay women, especially married women, less than male employees who are doing the same job.)

This book posits that for a reward to be equitable, it must be at least somewhat based on past performance. To be efficient, it must play a role in catalyzing future performance. Sometimes the same reward can do both, but when this is not the case, one of the most fundamental choices any designer of reward systems must make is between equity and efficiency. (The difficulties associated with this trade-off were illustrated in my earlier discussion of the reward systems in use during World War II, Vietnam, and the war in Iraq.)

Two examples of sacrificing equity for efficiency come from the world of sports. The first concerns the U.S. professional sports drafts, which award selection rights to the teams in inverse order of their performance during the prior year. The process is inequitable to the high performers, but efficiently achieves its purpose of increasing future parity. A second, marvelous example of a reward whose efficiency derives directly from its gross inequity comes from *Sports Illustrated*: "When one of his players was late to practice, the coach would sit him down in the middle of the gym with a cold drink in his hand, while his team members (who hadn't done anything wrong) ran laps around him." The inequity in this case is immediate and obvious. The offsetting gain in future efficiency can be expected to take effect as soon as the latecomer's teammates have had a chance to tell him how they feel about their experience.

In work settings this trade-off comes into play when a firm promotes someone who has performed well but will be a poor leader (equity), promotes an average performer with proven leadership skills (efficiency), or fills the position from the outside by offering more than what comparable insiders are getting (efficiency). As another example, many companies compensate people according to their length of service or rely on across-the-board adjustments (e.g., freezing everyone's budget or increasing everyone's compensation by 10 percent). These practices may or may not be equitable, depending on your definition of equity. They are obviously inefficient, however, because they will not cause anything good to happen.

Trade-off 2: Rewarding performance versus attendance versus seniority. In every organization people's compensation is primarily influenced by three factors: (1) What job do they have? (Managers typically earn more than supervisors, colonels more than captains, and full professors more than associates.)

(2) How long have they done it? (3) How well have they done it? Now, suppose I was only allowed to ask two questions and then had to guess how much your people are earning. Which question is least useful to predict your people's pay? Your response will probably vary for different employees and different locations. Unions often oppose even the smallest performance-based incentives, so your unionized operations are likely to be dominated by question 2. Governmental agencies (including the U.S. House and Senate) also tend to distribute rewards on the basis of seniority. Question 3 is more predictive in some cultures than others. American corporations, for example, make rewards more performance contingent than do companies in Scandinavia and Japan. Considerable variance also exists with respect to question 1. In investment banks and trading firms, the title of *analyst* may reveal little about compensation, whereas in many universities your title (and the name of your chair or professorship) is the primary determinant of pay, prestige, and job content rewards.

Most organizations set out to reward performance, but if their metrics aren't up to the task (or if it feels like too much work), they unintentionally reward attendance—coming in every day, being on time, looking busy—instead. They may not intend to reward attendance; they just may not be aware that they're doing so. For example, here's the pay-for-performance system that endured for many years in one of America's largest insurance companies:

- If an employee was outstanding (a select category into which no more than two employees per section could be placed): 5 percent salary increase

- If an employee was above average (all employees who were not outstanding were routinely placed in this category): 4 percent

- If an employee committed gross acts of negligence or incompetence, for which he would be fired in many other firms: 3 percent

- However, if an employee was late or absent three times in any six-month period: no increase at all

If rewarding attendance proves too daunting, the organization begins to reward membership. Membership rewards are either fixed—everyone gets them when they join—or variable, meaning that the longer you're a member, the more of the reward you receive.

I am not arguing that all rewards should be distributed on the basis of performance. Other factors do matter but should not be permitted to overwhelm or substitute for performance. Dispensing rewards without concern for performance is a great example of rewarding the wrong things and is particularly upsetting to your most productive employees. One of the golden rules of management is, never hurt your high performers. This rule may seem obvious, but it's often violated. I noted earlier that high performers are less likely than low performers to be given performance feedback. Poor performers can also take vacations and college courses when they want and are far more likely to be offered lucrative incentives to retire early. As another example, across-the-board budget cuts are more painful for high performers than for corporate politicians (who build slack into their budgets as a hedge) and incompetent leaders (who manage their operations so poorly that there's plenty of fat to cut). Across-the-board raises are also generally undesirable, which is made worse by the fact that organizations usually employ them at exactly the wrong time—that is, when times are hard and there's not enough money to go around. The motive for doing so is to equitably share the pain, but equity in such cases comes at the high cost of diminished efficiency. If you're going to distribute money aimlessly, do it when you have a lot, not when there's barely enough to take care of your high performers.

Remember, in general, what you reward is what you get. If you reward seniority, you are likely to get very little in the way of risk taking, innovation, and candid upward feedback. If you reward attendance, employees will leave their sports jackets on their chairs and their cars in the parking lot and carpool home. But if you reward high performance in the manner described in this book, there's an excellent chance you'll get it.

Trade-off 3: Rewarding individuals versus teams. Individual rewards are uniquely powerful. Telling someone, "If you perform well, you'll receive a bonus" is more motivating than saying, "If the company does well, you'll receive a bonus." Why? Because he has far more control over his own performance than the company's. Rewarding people for outcomes they can't influence is akin to buying your employees dinner if York defeats Essex. Though it may cause them to root ardently for the organization, it will not improve the likelihood of success. On the other hand, individual rewards tend to discourage mentoring, cross-marketing, and teamwork—because it takes time to share ideas and teach others, and because high performers often benefit from working alongside less competent colleagues who can't compete for the customer's business and the boss's favor. The key is to find the right balance.

In seeking the optimal balance between individual and team rewards, James Thompson, in his classic work *Organizations in Action*, is particularly helpful. Thompson identified three types of interdependence, of which the least complicated is pooled interdependence, whereby the performances of team members are aggregated to form a team score but each member can perform his assigned tasks without assistance from other members. Sports examples include golfers, tennis players, and bowlers. Workplace examples include salespeople with exclusive territories, stock pickers and programmers who work alone, and telecommuters who work at home. Sequential interdependence also allows people to do their jobs independently, but A's outputs become B's inputs, B's outputs are inputs for C, and so on. Most assembly-line work is of this kind, and so is a great deal of white-collar work and swimming and track relays. In the most complicated type of interdependence, reciprocal, there is no set work flow; team members react to each other simultaneously. Examples include medical teams during surgery, race-car crews during a pit stop, and football, basketball, and hockey players.

When interdependence is pooled, individual rewards (and individual goals and metrics) are often desirable. If you tell a golfer, "I'll give you $500 for each stroke below 85," he is likely to practice harder and take the next round more seriously. If he later tells you, "I shot 110, but I can explain," do you have to listen to his explanation? No, because when interdependence is pooled, each person can be held accountable for his own performance. However, individual rewards provide no incentive for golfers to correct each other's strokes and exchange tips about the course. If you believe your golfers have valuable information to share, you might want to offer an additional bonus to the entire team if they win the match.

Now let's consider basketball, which I said is a reciprocally interdependent sport. If you tell a basketball player, "I'll give you $500 for every point you score," he's likely to engage in self-serving behaviors that hurt the team. The bonus may also be inequitable because, unlike the golfer, the basketball player must depend on his teammates to achieve his goals and may fail through no fault of his own. Offering the same bonus to the other team members will only make matters worse. The problem is that, by offering individual rewards in circumstances where teamwork is essential, you're rewarding the wrong things.

The tendency to search for individual heroes and villains, even in reciprocal interdependence situations, is deeply ingrained in American culture. No Super Bowl or basketball championship tournament can end without identifying the star of the game or the most valuable player. Similarly, when something goes wrong in business, the first reaction from an American CEO is often, "Who did this? Bring me anyone!" Conversely, the Japanese are as fond of disguising accountability as we are of locating it. (One consequence of group decision making is that no one loses face if things turn out badly.) It's not by coincidence that the Americans teach their children that "the early bird gets the worm," while Japanese children are learning that "the nail that sticks up is the nail that gets hammered down."

Trade-off 4: Rewards versus punishment. This book is focused on rewards, with only passing references to punishment. Why? Because punishment is an ineffective way to change behavior. First, it tends to alienate people. Some managers say, "I'm not here to be loved; I'm here to get the work done," but that misses the point, which is that alienating people is expensive. Absences, lateness, and grievances increase, for example, and morale and job satisfaction decrease. Second, whereas rewards increase the likelihood that someone will do what you want, punishment gets someone to stop doing something you don't want and leaves open the mystery of what he'll do instead. He may now do what you want or may do something else you don't care for. For example, my high school grades were so bad that the only college that would accept me was far from my house, so sometimes I was late for my first class. To punish lateness, the professor would stop her lecture in midsentence and glare at us until we took our seats. Because we were all afraid of her, the only seats available to latecomers were, of course, in the first row of a large auditorium, so the journey took a long, long time. Though the professor was hoping for promptness, what she got instead was absence, because when we knew we would be late, my friends and I would skip class altogether.

On the other hand, there's an old saying that "you can't beat something with nothing." Sometimes rewards are unavailable or are determined by seniority or other factors beyond your control. In such cases punishment may be the only tool you have to get your people's attention.

Telling the Truth

In this book I have sought to describe and analyze a wide variety of dysfunctional reward systems that, unfortunately, constitute common practice in most universities, hospitals, government agencies, and social service organizations, as well as in the military, sports, and business. In closing this section, I'd like to take a brief look at a particularly dysfunctional reward system—namely, the tendency for many organizations, in all realms of human activity, to urge people to communicate honestly and then punish them when they do. Of all reward system anomalies, this may well be the worst, often causing organization members to become highly stressed and disillusioned, and sometimes even putting them at legal risk.

As an example of punishing candor, many managers exhort their subordinates to be upbeat and positive, and regard any pessimistic forecast or disagreement about policy as an act of disloyalty. Of course, the unethical employees aren't put off by such exhortations. They simply figure out what behaviors are rewarded, and that's what they do. ("My boss only wants to hear good news. I bring him good news. What's the problem?") It's the ethical people, those who care about the organization and want to do the right thing, who are stressed by systems that punish them when they act responsibly. Being honest in one's performance reviews is often similarly discouraged. In one of my classes at Michigan, a senior naval officer told the class that he had once submitted a set of performance reviews that identified the weaknesses as well as the strengths of his subordinates, only to learn that this caused them to be ranked lower than nearly everyone else of similar rank in the navy. Not only had he jeopardized his people's careers by being honest; he had put himself at risk, as evidenced by a note from his boss urging him to do something about the widespread personnel problems in his unit. He told the class at Michigan, "I may be slow, but I'm not stupid." He went on to say that the following year he labeled all his people as high performers and received another note from his boss, saying how pleased he was with the rapid improvement in the unit's effectiveness.

In politics, too, we want people to be candid and then usually punish them when they are. For example, we would like to know before an election which programs each candidate will pursue, how they will be funded, and which programs will be put on the back burner. Yet we punish (i.e., withhold support from) politicians who provide such information while rewarding those who promise free health care and quality education for everyone, with nary a clue about where the money will come from.

Ironically, one of the most meticulous efforts ever devised to reward candor has, in some cases, become a parody of the ills it was meant to correct. I'm referring to the decision to reward whistle-blowers by giving them, in some cases, a percentage of the money the organization has been losing to pilferage, fraud, or embezzlement. The result, probably not to your surprise, is that some whistle-blowers have put off blowing their whistles for quite a while and have even participated in the illegal activity to run up their take.

What to Do Monday Morning

I hope the ideas expressed to this point have been of interest to you and that you may want to try out a few of them in your own organization. This final section offers a few suggestions about how to get started.

Measure Early in the Cycle

Yes, it's best to start measuring things early in the process, but measuring for the sake of measuring isn't helpful. To measure what matters, consider the following advice.

Don't Confuse Activities with Outcomes

The problem with long-term performance is that it doesn't show up for a while. While they wait, most organizations overattend to measures of short-term performance and to activities. Activity metrics are often useful as lead indicators of performance but frequently are confused with performance itself; then they're rewarded for their own sake, with unfortunate consequences.

At the start of a new initiative, organizations measure and report on things that don't tell you much about anything. For example, I'm guessing that the most recent birth announcement you received contained the following information: name, gender, date of birth, length, and weight. That's it. Was important information left out? No. There *isn't* any other information. When GE's Work-Out program was born, we proudly announced the number of workshops we held, the number of employees who attended, how many ideas were generated, and the percentage of ideas that were implemented. Did these data provide insight into the value of the program? Not really, though they did convey some sense of whether people were getting into the game. Similarly, during the early stages of GE's Six Sigma initiative, we reported the number of people who earned certification, and at what level—brown belt, black belt, etc.,—they were certified. We announced the number of projects that were started and what stage each project was in. Unfortunately, what happened in both cases—GE being as results oriented as it is—was that these activities came to be regarded as ends in themselves. Some of the businesses began to compete to see who could run the most Work-Out workshops with the most people. (The winning business ran a workshop every week with eighty-five to ninety people in attendance, which wasn't very productive.) Similarly, in their zest to create Six Sigma black belts and projects, more than one GE business diluted the criteria to earn a black belt and also reduced the requirements for how projects got certified.

The right approach is to make use of activity metrics as lead indicators of performance, keeping in mind that they are mere activities, not results. It may be useful to offer some (small, preferably nonfinancial) rewards to people or departments whose results are outstanding, but these rewards should not be so attractive that people begin to focus their attention on the activities rather than on the performance those activities are supposed to catalyze.

Identify Some Local Heroes

At the start of a new initiative, your existing metrics may not be sensitive enough to tell you how well each of your people is currently performing in the area you're trying to improve. However, you should be able to recognize a best practice, if one exists within your organization, or an outstanding achievement. Therefore, when you launch your initiative, you should seek to honor and celebrate the accomplishments of one or more of your people who already excel at the desired new behaviors. To focus attention on cross-marketing, for example, Goldman Sachs gave out awards to several employee teams that had created significant cross-marketing opportunities. At this early stage it is usually not helpful to put the spotlight on people whose performance is poor. Later, once more reliable metrics are in place, you can begin to hold each person accountable for how well, or how poorly, he is achieving the desired outcomes.

Run in Parallel

Sometimes an initiative is driven by an urgent need— for example, discovering that you're out of compliance with some new regulation—and you must move quickly. Often, however, you can increase people's receptivity toward a change by creating a safe period to practice the desired new behaviors. Examples of this practice include preseason in sports, previewing plays in New Haven before they go to Broadway, and the self-study period preceding an Association to Advance Collegiate Schools of Business audit (described earlier). When I have created such a safe period, either with my own staff or as a consultant, I usually say something like this: "We've designed a new compensation system (or cross-marketing formula, or performance evaluation process) to replace the one we're using now. We believe it's a better system, but new systems always have glitches, and it wouldn't be fair to put you at risk while we get the bugs out. Therefore, we're going to calculate your earnings both ways—using the existing approach and the new one—and you'll receive whichever amount is higher. However, once the new system is working properly, we're going to start using it, so please take this opportunity to begin to share ideas (or improve your cold-calling, or text-messaging skills, or whatever is required to excel under the new system)."

Diagnose Your Organization's Reward System

I have spoken at length about many organizations' tendency to discourage the behaviors they need while rewarding the very actions that are driving them out of business. Here are two simple tests you can use to see whether the problems I have described are prevalent in your organization. The first of these pertains to whether you are rewarding things in the right way, the second to whether you are rewarding the right things.

Are You Rewarding Things Right?

First, list your organization's rewards (and don't forget your prestige and job content rewards) down the side of a page, and put eligibility, reversibility, and the other tests I've discussed across the top, making a grid. Then, taking each box in the grid one by one, ask the following questions:

- Is this reward passing the test?

- If it's failing, do you want it to fail? (For example, we've noted that organizations usually prefer that their financial rewards not be visible.)

- If you don't like the fact that the reward is failing, how can you change the reward, or the way you administer the award, so that it passes the test? For example, how could you make the reward more reversible, more performance contingent, or more timely? How might you improve its visibility or increase the number of people eligible to receive it?

You can conduct this exercise by yourself, but you'll get better information and more buy-in if you involve employees from different functions and departments and at different levels.

Are You Rewarding the Right Things?

We noted earlier that the clean sheet exercise permits you to assess the fit between your existing metrics and the metrics required to be responsive to stakeholder demands. This next exercise is a great test of the fit between the behaviors you say you want and the behaviors your employees say you're rewarding.

If you like, you can use the output from the bull's-eye exercise—the behaviors in the center—as inputs to this exercise. If you haven't done the bull's-eye exercise, the first step is to make a list of behaviors you'd like to see more of and a list of behaviors you'd like to see less of. Next, randomly combine items from the two lists into a single list of behaviors, as in figure 2.

Now ask your people to rate each behavior, using the key in figure 2. You can ask them to respond online, or you can make the results anonymous by mailing the survey to their homes or putting a box for completed surveys in the employee lounge or cafeteria. When you receive the data, make a list of those actions you would like to see more of, but that respondents say are ignored or punished, and behaviors you want less of, but which they say are rewarded.

I have done this exercise in numerous organizations and found that employee descriptions of their

FIGURE 2

Rewarding the right items

Using the following choices, please indicate what would be most likely to happen if you were to do each of the actions described below:

1 = The action would usually bring reward or approval.
2 = The action would probably bring neither approval nor disapproval.
3 = The action would probably bring punishment or disapproval.
4 = Response to this action is unpredictable, ranging from approval to disapproval.

☐ Coming up with and trying out new, untested ideas

☐ Exceeding your authority when necessary to get the job done

☐ Bending the rules when necessary to get the job done

☐ Violating the chain of command when necessary to get the job done

☐ Going along with the boss even when he or she is wrong

☐ Always going along with the majority view

☐ Presenting your boss with an unpopular point of view

☐ Sharing information with other units and departments

☐ Keeping information from other units and departments

☐ Achieving your group's goals at the expense of other groups

☐ Setting very easy goals and then achieving them

☐ Maximizing the short-term bottom line at the expense of the long-term bottom line reward systems inevitably deteriorate as you descend the hierarchy. Executives near the top usually report that their rewards pass most of the tests of a good reward system and that the organization rewards candor, innovation, risk taking, and other behaviors they consider desirable. Lower-level employees, however, tend to see things differently. I'm not saying that these people are correct, but if they're right, you have an action item, and if they're wrong, you still have an action item. For example, many people at GE felt that Jack Welch punished push-back. I worked for him for a long time and think that isn't true. However, it doesn't matter what I think. What does matter is that the people who believed it didn't push back, so Welch suffered the same consequence—the loss of potentially useful information—as if it were true. So don't become defensive about the data. If you disagree with your people's perceptions, you should engage them in a free-flowing dialogue to find out why they feel that way. If you think they may be reluctant to speak up, you might start the discussion by saying something like this: "I'm not asking how you, personally, replied to any of the survey questions. I'm trying to understand why 34 percent of your colleagues feel that 'going the extra mile for the customer' is punished and why only 53 percent believe that 'coming up with new ideas' is rewarded." I have found that, presented this way, even nervous people participate, sometimes by saying, "I don't feel that way myself, but maybe this is what some of my associates may have been thinking about when they answered."

Some Good News About Rewards

Let me end this book with three optimistic comments and an observation. First, I've tried to show that most organizations' reward and measurement systems are inconsistent with even the most basic principles. If this is true in your organization, your opportunities for improvement are tremendous. Second, the odds are excellent that your competitors' systems are badly flawed, which provides you with a great chance to gain competitive advantage. Third, remember that the power of a reward is unrelated to its cost. The key to improving the effectiveness of your reward system is not to add head count, hire consultants, or upgrade your IT capabilities but to define, measure, and reward performance in a manner that is consistent with the principles discussed in this book.

Now the observation: even though your organization may not be adhering to the principles, you may well be doing what I've been recommending—at home! Consider the following examples:

- You're renting a house. You hate the house, and you hate the people who are renting you the house. You're obligated by the contract to mow the lawn. (You hate the lawn.) The neighbors' kid offers to cut the grass. Do you pay him by the job or by the hour? By the job. The kid may do good work if he has a thing for lawns, but you've given him no reason to, so he is likely to do a quick, slip-shod job. This is fine with you, since you hate the lawn. Afterward, you wouldn't complain about the work ethic of young people today, because you haven't learned anything about the work ethic of young people today. If you'd wanted a good job you could have paid the kid by the hour; overpaid him by the hour, in which case each blade would probably be razor-cut; or told him, "You get your money after I inspect the lawn."

- You tell your children that they can't go to the mall until their room is clean. Your kids don't much care if their room is clean (they know where everything is), but that's OK; you don't much care if they go to the mall. Nevertheless, because you've made their goal attainment contingent on your goals, established a pertinent metric, and made your reward visible, timely, and performance contingent, there's a definite possibility that they will clean their room.

- You ask your overly competitive son to cut the cake and inform him that his sister will select the first piece. This is reminiscent of the system Jack Welch put in place to ensure that his would-be successors wouldn't engage in dysfunctional behavior. He made no attempt to alter their goal-driven, competitive nature. Instead, he created a framework and a set of guidelines that provided incentives to collaborate with one another (similar to the boy in our example, who will endeavor mightily to cut the cake into pieces of exactly the same size).

In these examples, you did not assume that other people care about the same things you care about, nor did you blame them for having needs and preferences that are different from your own. Instead, you used the promise of prospective rewards to induce other people to care about some things that are important to you.

Our work organizations are larger and far more complex, but the principles are the same.

Good luck.

About the Author

Now a Senior Advisor to Goldman Sachs, Steve Kerr was for six years the firm's chief learning officer. Prior to that, he spent seven years as GE's vice president of corporate leadership development and CLO, including responsibility for GE's renowned leadership education center at Crotonville. Steve was previously on the business school faculties of Ohio State, the University of Michigan, and the University of Southern California, where he was Dean of the Faculty and director of the PhD program. Dr. Kerr is a former president of the Academy of Management, the world's largest association of academicians in management. His writings on leadership, including the Academy of Management article "On the Folly of Rewarding A, While Hoping for B," are among the most cited and reprinted in the management sciences.

Steve has acted as a consultant to many of the world's largest corporations. His many board memberships include the board of directors of Harvard

About the Author

Business School Publishing and the board of directors of The Motley Fool. He is a senior advisory committee member to the U.S. Department of Homeland Security, and is Chairman of the Board of the Fisher Island (Florida) Day School, under the erratic supervision of his five year old son Zachary.